EXCEL

2022

Excel Made Easy
The Ultimate Crash Course to Master Excel Without Getting Overwhelmed
Secret Winning Formulas to Stand Out from the Crowd and Impress Your
Boss

D1607064

by Max Clark

💣A GIFT FOR YOU 💣

In this book, I am excited to offer you 3 free bonuses that will take your Excel skills to the next level.

At the end of this book, as a token of my appreciation for investing in your Excel proficiency, you will find your exclusive gift which contains the below topics:

Bonus 1: Top 30 Excel Interview Questions for 2023 (Beginner to Advanced)

Bonus 2: The Top 5 Mistakes everybody makes when using Excel and why they are stopping you from advancing your Excel level.

Bonus 3: The #1 Secret that I used to quickly advance my Excel skills

By taking advantage of this bonus, you will not only improve your Excel skills but also increase your value to your employer or clients. I hope you find these resources to be a valuable addition to your Excel toolkit.

Max

TABLE OF CONTENTS

INTRODUCTION

Excel is a database-like spreadsheet program. Large volumes of data may be organized and analyzed quickly and simply by using the individual cells in the spreadsheet. Using columns and rows, Excel allows you to store data in a logically ordered manner. Allows for the presentation of extensive data sets in an easy-to-understand manner. The corporate world's most used spreadsheet program is Microsoft Excel. All professions use Excel regularly: bankers, accountants, business analysts, marketers, scientists, or entrepreneurs. To remain competitive in today's global marketplace, all businesses must constantly adapt and innovate. Implementing training and development programs for staff is one method to keep on top of the newest technology and maximize revenue. Employers may safeguard their most important assets by ensuring their employees get ongoing training and growth opportunities.

A company's best workers desire to be stretched and work hard to maintain their leadership position. Employers may reduce employee turnover and the danger of losing their best employees to the competition by offering them the ongoing education they require to be productive as they aspire to be. This educational instruction often includes Microsoft Excel for Business. What is the purpose of Excel? Excel permits users to organize, analyze, & assess mathematical data, enabling managers & senior executives to make significant options that might directly impact the firm. They can better communicate their data to senior management if they are schooled in sophisticated Excel functionalities. It's also a must-have ability for those aiming to get to the top of their respective organizations. Both individuals and employers may profit from learning advanced Excel. Let's take a closer look at the benefits of using Excel as part of a company's regular staff training program.

After reading this guide, you'll get a firm grasp of the fundamentals of Excel, including what it is, how it works, the most useful functions, and formulae. To progress in your work, you must keep learning and improving your abilities. There are certain important abilities that advanced Excel emphasizes, and these talents may be put to good use in every position within a firm. After learning this guide, you must be able to: Visualize, modify, and assess the data. Improve the productivity of your workflow, projects, financial predictions, and budgets by developing equations that may help you collect more data. Provide senior management with an easy-to-understand collection of facts to analyze current projects or conditions at the organization. Create spreadsheets that make it easier to enter data and show it more meaningfully. The ability to decipher information in spreadsheets and from third-party providers and customers. Help the company by being capable of unraveling more complex data and finding solutions to its difficulties. Complicated financial and inventory records must be kept in order and balanced. Work with multiple departments and activities to develop tracking systems considering the diverse workflows involved.

So, it would help if you started this amazing journey of learning from basic to advanced features of excel that can help you grow in your professional and personal life.

CHAPTER 1: GETTING STARTED WITH MICROSOFT EXCEL

Information may be stored, sorted, and analyzed with the help of Excel, a spreadsheet tool. Excel's tremendous features aren't only for experts; despite popular belief, anybody can learn to utilize them to their advantage. Excel simplifies working with many kinds of data, whether you're maintaining a budget, arranging a learning log, or making an invoice.

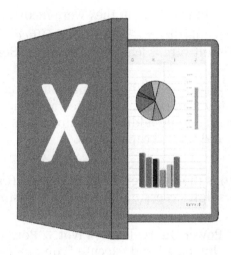

1.1 MICROSOFT OFFICE OVERVIEW (VERSIONS OF EXCEL)

From 1985 up till now, there have been thirty versions of MS Excel. Most users use Excel 2016, Excel 2019, Excel 2021, or Excel 365. Excel has undergone major revisions with each release, and there are still notable differences between the Windows and Mac versions. The most recent version of Excel is what you should use to learn the program rather than an older version. The reason behind this is discussed in this chapter.

Excel 365

Excel 365 will live forever. Instead of a 3-year upgrade cycle, 365 adds new features with every edition.

Microsoft established "update channels" for Office 365 because corporate customers don't want continual change. Large corporations may choose six-monthly updates. This gave a tested "semi-annual" version in Jan and Jul. The Smart Method updates its books whenever Office 365 adds new functionality. In February 2022, Microsoft issued the sixth edition containing the Jan 2022 update. Only The Smart Method updates its products this way.

Excel 365 has gained numerous great features since 2019, but nothing compares to July 2020's Dynamic Arrays and functions. This change isn't minor. Excel's engine was rewritten to support dynamic arrays. Automatic Data Analysis & Natural Language Queries debuted in 2021. Expanded linked data types.

In Excel 365, many older functions behave differently, and array-aware functions have substituted several old favorites. LOOKUP replaces VLOOKUP.

Excel 365's new dynamic array feature surpassed Excel 2019. Dynamic arrays are incompatible with using Excel 2019 & will cause current (Excel 365) files to not operate in outdated versions. Excel 2021 has no trouble with dynamic arrays.

Excel 365 would be the newest, finest, and most capable Excel version & costs a small monthly fee.

Excel 2021

Many critics said Excel 2021 wouldn't exist, but they were incorrect again.

It's odd to offer another "perpetual license" edition of Office alongside Excel 365. Microsoft has adopted the SaaS model, where software is leased and not sold. Some buyers still favor the "buy once, use forever" strategy.

Many pundits believe Excel 2021 is the final perpetually licensed version. Excel 2021 is already far behind Excel 365, with connected data types, automated analysis, & Natural Language inquiries only accessible to Excel 365 customers. Some additional innovations are introduced to Excel 2021. Excel 2021 included dynamic arrays and related capabilities.

Excel 2019

Many critics believe Excel 2019 is the final perpetual license edition. Excel 2019 is already far behind Excel 365, with dynamic arrays only accessible to Excel 365 customers. No new additions have been introduced to Excel 2019.

All versions of Excel 2019 have Power Query, Power Pivot, & Power Maps (3D Maps). These high-level OLAP tools let Excel examine "big data" and execute "contemporary data analysis" on any version. "Power" tools have developed since MS Excel 2019 was published, providing more "power" capabilities accessible solely to Excel 365 customers.

Excel 2016 and Excel 2016 for the Office 365 Members

There were two major ways in which Excel 2016 diverged from earlier versions of the program:
While there are significant differences between the Mac & Windows versions, both are referred to as "Excel 2016." (Previous versions utilized different year numbers to avoid confusion).
If you subscribed to Office 365, you got updates automatically over the internet, which made the copy of "Excel 2016" different from the version used by those who didn't pay for the service.
For example, we had to constantly update our Excel 2016 book to accommodate both Excel 2016 & Excel 2016 for Office 365 users, making this a challenging Excel edition to provide instructional materials. The two diverged during the product's lifespan.
The Smart Method breathed a sigh of relief when subsequent releases clearly distinguished between Excel 2019 & Excel 365.

Excel 2016 & Excel 365 for Windows

As with Excel 2016, MS has started rolling out incremental improvements to the program's functionality via the internet rather than waiting until a major version update is issued. Users who purchased the boxed retail edition of Excel were left with a completely different version of the program than those who subscribed to Office 365, who had access to all the new features.

Excel 2016 for Mac

Microsoft decided to finally unify the Excel names for both Windows and Mac in 2016 with MS Excel 2016. However, the iOS operating system's unique user interface still separates these apps from one another.

Excel 2013 (Windows)

Excel 2013 included the Slicers, Flash Fill features, & 50 new functions; however, it was only available for Windows systems.

Excel 2011 (Mac)

The 2011 version of Excel is Mac-exclusive. Excel for Mac no longer shared its name with its Windows equivalent since this was the final version.

This was version 13 of Excel for Mac, much as Windows' Excel 2010; however, because of fear of the number 13, Excel 2011 was renamed version 14.

Excel 2010 (Windows)

Microsoft Excel 2010 is exclusive to Windows PCs. The new features it debuted were the multi-threaded support, sparklines, the ability to personalize the Ribbon, and a hidden "backstage" view. Because 13 is an unlucky number, Microsoft decided to bypass version 13 instead of labeling Excel 2010 as version 14.

Excel 2008 (Mac)

Excel 2008 had only been made available on computers manufactured by Apple.

Excel 2007 (Windows)

The 2007 version of Excel is exclusive to Windows PCs.

Excel 2007 was a major improvement over past versions, including new features like the Ribbon interface and a new file format that replaced the old.xls and xlsm files. With this update, Excel files gained the capacity to contain over one million rows (up from the previous maximum of 16,384) & received significant security upgrades. The Excel charting tools have also been upgraded significantly.

Even though surveys at the time indicated that most users disapproved of the Ribbon, Microsoft stuck with it, and now, those same people wouldn't want to return.

Excel 2004 (Mac)

Excel 2004 was made available only on Macs.

Excel 2003 (Windows)

The "Windows, Menus, Icons, Pointer" ('WIMP') user interface, which was used in earlier versions of Excel, was retired in Excel 2003. There were drop-down menus & icons up top that you'd recognize if you used it.

Tables were introduced in Excel 2003 and were further enhanced in subsequent versions.

Older Windows version (2002, 2000, 97, 95, 4.0, 3.0, 2.0)

Previous versions of Excel may be traced back to 1987 with the introduction of Excel 2.0. Excel's most recognizable features have been around for quite some time.

1992 saw the introduction of Excel 4.0, which included the initial version of the now-standard AutoFill feature.

Excel 5.0 was published in 1993, and it was then that VBA and Macros first appeared. As a result of VBA's adaptability, Excel was a prime target for macro infections until the release of Excel 2007, which introduced new file formats with enhanced protection.

Excel 97 introduced the Office Assistant "Clippy," but most workers found it very irritating. Excel 2002 had it turned off by default, while Excel 2007 got rid of it altogether.

Older Mac version (2001, 2000, 98, 5, 4, 3, 2, 1)

Microsoft had a spreadsheet software called Multiplan that ran on MS-DOS & other console operating systems before Excel was even published; nevertheless, this is a little-known fact.

Excel 2, first released for the Mac, was ported to Windows in the initial version of Excel.

Microsoft's Excel 2019 on Windows & Excel 2019 on Mac go by the same name, and this isn't the first time they've done so; in 2000, Excel was made available for both Windows and Mac under the same moniker.

OS/2 Version (2.2,2.3,3)

In 1985, Microsoft and IBM collaborated to create OS/2, an operating system. There were 3 editions of Excel for OS/2 before IBM completely took it over in 1992.

1.2 EXCEL USER INTERFACE

Microsoft Excel users' interface is not limited to the grid pattern of columns and rows described within Excel Spreadsheets.

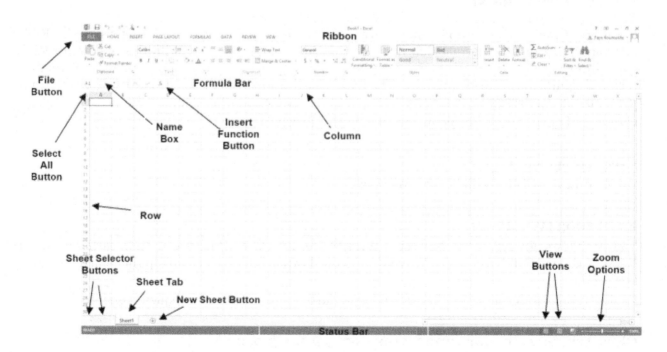

Interface Element	Description
Ribbon Tabs	Ribbon Tab is a tab that organizes commands by topic
The Ribbon	Commands underneath the Tabs
Ribbon Groups	Grouping of related commands
Dialog Box Launcher	Opens a dialog box that includes additional commands
Quick Access Toolbar	One click accesses to any frequently used command
Name Box	Displays cell location and can be used to navigate to a cell location
Select All Button	Selects all the cells in a worksheet
Formula Bar	View, enter, or edit cell contents
Insert Function Button	Displays Insert Function dialog box
Scroll Bars	Used to navigate up, down, left & right
Zoom Slider	Zoom into an area of the worksheet
View Buttons	Switch between Normal, Page Layout and Page Break Preview views
Worksheet tabs	Tabs used to select individual worksheets
The Workspace	The area inside of the columns and rows used in Excel
Columns	Columns use letters
Rows	Rows use numbers

Ribbon Overview

- **Home** - Standardized layout with access to standard features, common organization methods, and more.

- **Insert** - Use this section to enter various tables, figures, charts, hyperlinks, and other textual objects.

- **Page Layout** - Regarding Drawing Object Themes, Scaling, Page Setup, Sheet Options, & Layout

- **Formula** - The Insert Function, Formula Auditing, Range Name, & Calculations Options

- **Data** - Data Tools, Filter/sort, and Outlining are all Database Options.

- **Review** - To Edit, Comment, Safeguard, and Keep Track of Changes

- **View** - Indicators for Views, Hide/Show, Zoom, Window Controls, & Macros in a Worksheet

1.3 EXCEL WORKBOOK

Workbooks are the common name for Excel files. In Excel, a new workbook must be created for each new project. Excel 2016 provides several entry points for beginning work on a worksheet.

You may start from scratch when making a new workbook, or you can use one of several available templates.

Creating a blank workbook

Here are the procedures you need to take to create a brand new, empty workbook in Microsoft Excel: Start by going to the File menu, which will open the Excel Backstage window.

Followed by clicking New, followed by Blank workbook.

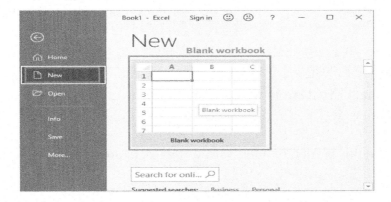

Here, a brand-new, empty spreadsheet will be generated automatically.

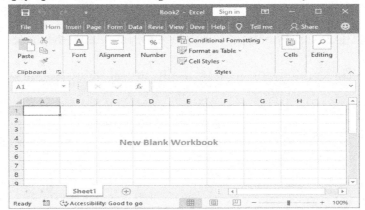

Open your existing workbook

You won't only be making new workbooks but also opening ones that have been saved. Data may already be present in an existing worksheet. It may be opened either in its native format or in Microsoft Excel. Just do what's written down here:

From the File menu, choose Backstage view, and then click Open.

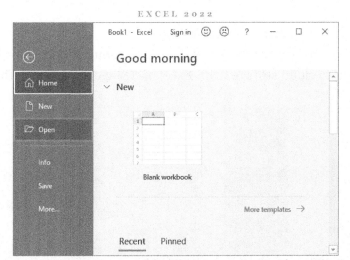

You can now use Microsoft Excel to access previously saved files from your local hard drives or your cloud storage space (OneDrive) under the "Recent" tab.

Opening an existing file from your local storage

Click your Browse option to choose an already-existing file from your computer.

The Open box will pop up, and you may access your computer's local storage. Find the file you want to open, then press the Open button.

The Employee worksheet, found on the Desktop, has been opened.

Opening your files from your cloud storage

Follow these procedures to access your Excel file from a cloud service like OneDrive:

To access your OneDrive cloud storage from Excel backstage area, follow these steps:

If you haven't already, sign in to the OneDrive account.

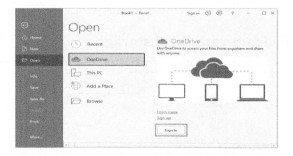

Now, access the existing file saved on the cloud storage.

You may save time by looking through your recently used workbooks instead of searching for the one you're looking for if you've opened it in the last few days.

Opening your existing files from the Recent files

In Excel, a Recent folder is available in the program's settings. It remembers recently seeing documents in a cache. Follow these instructions to access the included Excel file:

Click Open in Excel's backstage area, then locate the file you wish to open in Recent.

Pin your workbook

If you use the same worksheet often, you may "pin" it to your Backstage view so you can easily retrieve it.The first step is to open the "Backstage" window by clicking the "Open" button. Your revised workbooks are set in stone.

Second, you need to move the cursor over the desired spreadsheet before you can pin it. In the new window, a pin icon will appear next to the worksheet. Follow the on-screen instructions and choose the pin.

The workbook may be retrieved via the Recent Workbook or even the Pinned tab. Simply re-click the pushpin button to remove the workbook from the pinboard.

Compatibility mode

You may be working with a version of Excel many years old, like Excel 2003 and Excel 2000, and you have some files from that version lying around. Those worksheets need your attention and modification sometimes. The Compatibility view will be activated automatically when you open a file of this kind.

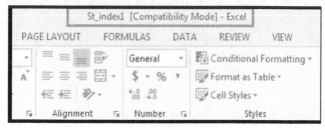

When you switch to compatibility mode, certain functions may be disabled. If a file was originally produced in Excel 2003, for instance, then just the tabs and instructions from that version of Excel will be accessible. As a result, you can only utilize the functions in the software that generated the worksheet.

To leave Compatibility mode, you must update the worksheet to the most updated version type. It's recommended to keep the worksheet in Compatibility mode if you're collaborating with people who are still using an older version of Excel.

For converting your workbook

You may convert the worksheet to the format used by the most recent version of Excel if you want to use all the enhancements in that program. For instance, update a workbook from an earlier version to the Current format.

If you want to open an older Excel file, follow these procedures.

1. Select the Information panel on the left side of the Excel Backstage screen.

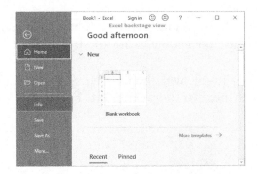

To do this, go to your Help menu, choose to Check for Issue, and then select Check Compatibility.

Compatibility issues with the current file will appear here. Click OK after selecting an Excel version.

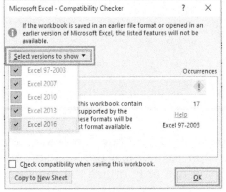

Open Save As. Choose where to store the workbook, name the presentation file, then click Save.

Your workbook will be updated.

Saving & Sharing Workbooks

When you create your new Excel worksheet, you'll need to save it so you may change it later. You may save Excel files locally, as in earlier versions. Excel 2016 and later versions save workbooks to OneDrive, unlike prior versions.

Excel can export & share workbooks.

Save & Save As

Save & Save As is Excel's file-saving option. These solutions are similar yet have key distinctions.

- **Save:** Save is used to save changes while creating or editing a worksheet. This is your main command.

- The first time you save a file, you must choose a location and a name. Click Save to save this with a similar location and name. Ctrl+S works too.

- **Save As:** This command duplicates the original worksheet. You must change the copy's name and location when using Save As.

Steps for saving your workbook

You must save your workbook when you start your new project or alter an existing one. Saving frequently prevents lost work.

1. Open your Quick Access Toolbars and choose Save.

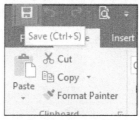

2. The Save As window appears in Backstage when saving a file for the first time. Choose a location and rename your file.

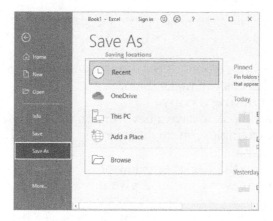

3. Click Browse to save the worksheet. Click OneDrive to save the file there.

The Save As dialogue box will appear at this point. Your workbook will be saved in a local storage area. To save the worksheet, type in the file name and click Save.

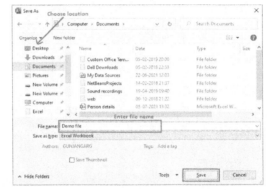

A copy of the spreadsheet will be stored. A Save command (Ctrl + S) may be used again to save your modifications to the worksheet as you make them.

Using your Save As for making a copy

Create a duplicate of the workbook to save a new version while maintaining the original. If you had a file called "Sales Data," for example, you might save this as "Sales Data-2" so that we can modify the new file & still refer to the original.

Select a Save As button within the Backstage view of the currently open file. If you are doing this 1st time, just choose a location to save your data & give this a new filename.

Auto Recover

While working in an Excel spreadsheet, it automatically saves it to a temporary folder. Excel Auto Recover lets you recover a file if you've forgotten to save your modifications or if your Excel crashes.

Using Auto Recover

1. Open the Latest version of Excel. The Document Recovery window will appear if any previous file versions have been auto saved.

2. Click on a file to open it. You'll get the workbook back.

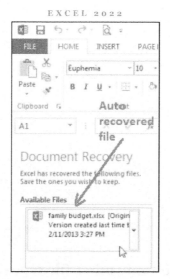

Using the Backstage view, you may go through all your AutoSaved files to find the one we're looking for. Look at the Help menu, then choose to Recover Unsaved Workbooks. You may configure the needed auto-recovery option from this point on.

Exporting Workbooks

Excel files are saved in the.xlsx file format by default. A PDF and Excel 97-2003 workbook may be appropriate in certain situations. Excel allows us to export your workbook in several file formats.

Exporting your workbook as a PDF file

A PDF file might be very useful if you want to share your workbook with someone who doesn't have Adobe Acrobat installed on their computer. Your workbook may be viewed but not edited by recipients using a PDF.

To open the Backstage view, first, click the File tab. Export, then choose the option to create PDF/XPS.

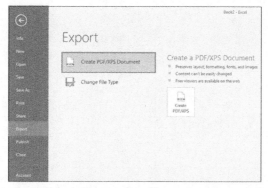

You'll see the Save As dialogue box open. Enter the file name you want to save and click the Publish button.

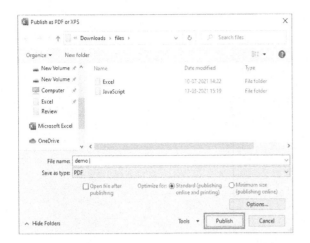 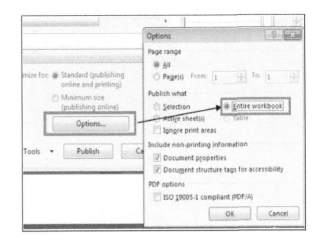

Exporting your workbook into some other file types

If you need to share your worksheet with someone using an earlier version of Excel, you may want to consider exporting it as Excel 97-2003 Workbook or a. If you require a plain-text workbook edition, you may use a CSV file instead.

To open the Backstage view, choose File from the View menu.

Click Export, then choose a different kind of file from the drop-down menu that appears.

Click Save As after choosing a popular file format.

A dialogue window called Save As will pop up. Click Save after deciding where to save the workbook and giving it a filename.

CHAPTER 2: BASIC FEATURES OF EXCEL

In this chapter, you will learn some basic features of excel including spreadsheets, understanding of rows and columns, conditional formatting, other users the features, feature excel and how you can import and export data in your excel file.

2.1 UNDERSTANDING EXCEL SPREADSHEET

There is at least one worksheet in each workbook. It would help if you created several worksheets to better arrange your workbook and make finding things easier when working with a sizable amount of data. You may also group worksheets to apply data to several worksheets at once.

Rename worksheet

One Sheet1 worksheet comes with a modern Excel workbook when you create it. The name of a worksheet may be altered to describe more accurately what's on it.

- Right-click each worksheet you want to rename, then choose the worksheet menu.

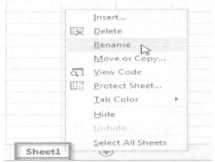

Name the worksheet you wish to use in the appropriate field.

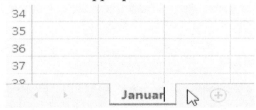

Press Enter or use your computer and mouse to travel outside your worksheet. The name of the spreadsheet would be modified.

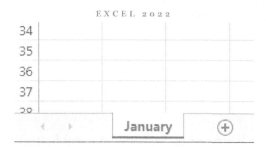

Insert a new worksheet

Click your new sheet key when you find it.

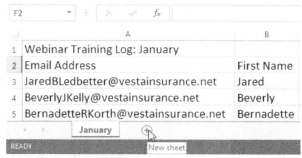

The screen would display a fresh, empty worksheet.

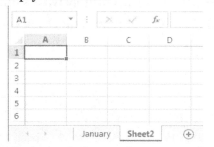

Go to Backstage preview, touch Options, and choose the appropriate number of worksheets for each new workbook to change the default workbook count.

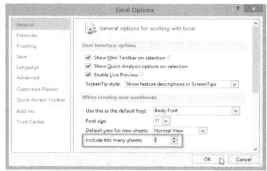

Delete worksheet

When you right-click on a worksheet you want to get rid of, you'll get an option to Delete it.

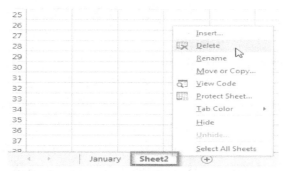

The worksheet on your spreadsheet will be removed.

When you right-click on a worksheet, you can choose Protect sheet from the worksheet menu to keep it from being edited or destroyed.

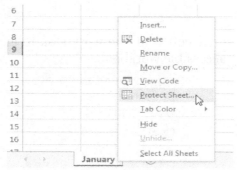

Copy worksheet

The contents of one worksheet may be copied to another using Excel's help.

Right-click the worksheet you want to copy and choose "Move or Transfer" from the worksheet menu.

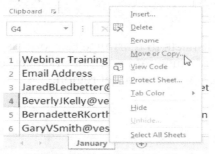

The "Move / Copy" dialogue box would display. Specify the location of your sheet in this field. The worksheet will be moved to the right of the present one (move toward the end).

Please click OK after selecting "Create a copy" from the drop-down menu."

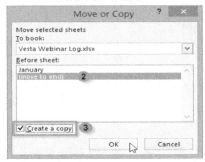

It will be possible to duplicate the worksheet. Your scenario's clone would have the same name & version number as the original worksheet since you copied it from a January worksheet (2). This month's data came from the January (1) worksheet and was carried over to the January (2) worksheet.

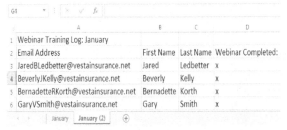

It is also possible to copy a worksheet from one workbook to another. The book drop-down menu allows you to choose from any accessible workbook.

Move worksheet

You may have to swap out worksheets to rearrange the spreadsheet. Select the worksheet you'd want to edit. You may see the cursor change into a little worksheet icon. Keep an eye out for a little black arrow once you've kept your cursor on the target region.

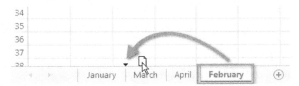

Release the mouse button. The worksheet has been moved to a new location.

Change the worksheet tab color

Change the color of a worksheet page to better organize your worksheets and make your workbook more user-friendly. After right-clicking on a worksheet tab, hover your mouse over the Tab color. The screen would show a color selection option. Pick a color that you like. As you move your mouse over different options, a sample of the most recent worksheet tab color will show. An example of this is Red.

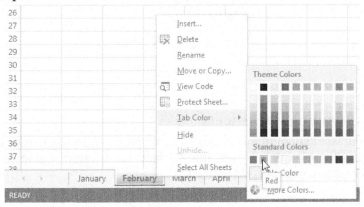

The tabs' color will be changed on the worksheet.

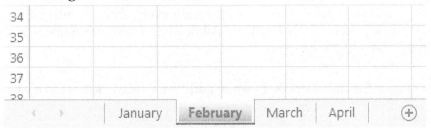

When you choose a worksheet, you'll see that the worksheet tab's color has faded dramatically. You can notice how the color changes if you choose another worksheet.

Switching between worksheets

Clicking the tab will take you to a different worksheet. If your workbook is large, you may find this time-consuming since you will have to search through each tab individually. Using the lower-left corner of the screen's scroll arrows to navigate instead is better.

There will be an appearance of a dialogue box with a list of all the sheets in the workbook in it. Once you've done that, double-click the sheet you wish to go to.

Grouping and ungrouping worksheets

You may work on one worksheet at a time, or you can work on many worksheets at once. It's possible to create a collection of worksheets by mixing worksheets. Changing one worksheet affects the other worksheets in the same category.

To group the worksheets:

In this instance, employees are required to be taught every three months. Because of this, you will create a separate worksheet category for them. Adding an employee's name to a spreadsheet will show up on all worksheets in the group.

Make sure you choose the first worksheet when adding a new worksheet to a category.

The Ctrl key on your keyboard should be held down.

From the drop-down menu, choose the next worksheet for the group. Select as many worksheets as you need to arrange before you stop.

The Ctrl key may be released. Groups have been created for your worksheets.

Once you've categorized the worksheets into a category, you may browse the worksheets in that category. Changes to one worksheet would be mirrored in the other worksheets for the group. If you want a worksheet that isn't a part of the community, you'll have to ungroup everything.

To ungroup all worksheets:

Right clicking a worksheet and selecting Un-group from the context menu will bring up the worksheet menu, from which you may choose sheets to print.

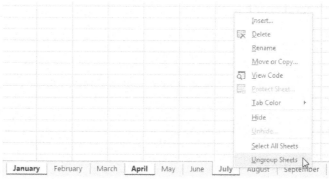

Groups of worksheets would be created. Instead, you may ungroup the worksheets by clicking on one of them.

Ungrouped and grouped worksheets are available. Group your January and March worksheets if you're following along with the scenario. Add fresh content to the January worksheet and compare it to the March worksheet.

Page Layout view
Open the worksheet in the Page Layout view to examine your layout modifications.
- Page Layout may be accessed by clicking on the command in the right-bottom corner of your worksheet.

Page Orientation
Excel supports two-page landscapes and portraits. Horizontal landscape, vertical portrait. The portrait is preferable for rows and the landscape for columns. When there are more rows than columns, portrait orientation works best.

Portrait   Landscape

To change page orientation:
- Select the Page Layout tab from the Ribbon.

- The Orientation drop-down box lets you choose between landscape and portrait.

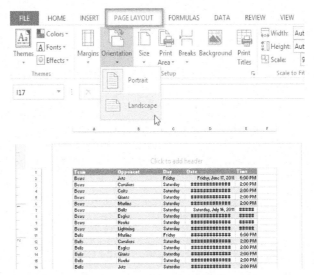

- The page orientation of the workbook will be changed.

To format page margins:

It's the space between the text and the page's margin. A one-inch space between the material on the page's boundaries and the default setting for every workbook. If your data doesn't fit on the page, you may need to adjust the margins. Excel has a variety of pre-set margin sizes from which you may choose.

- You may do this by clicking on the Page Layout menu on the Ribbon and selecting the Margins option.

- The margin size may be selected from the drop-down list. Narrow is an option to include more content on the page.

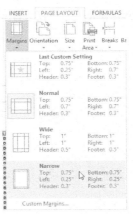

- In this case, the margins would be resized to fit your new selection.

To use custom margins:

The Page Setup dialogue box in Excel lets you choose the margin size.

- On the Page Layout tab, choose the Margins option and click OK. Custom Margins may be selected from the drop-down menu.

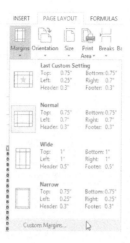

- Is there going to be a Page Setup dialogue box?

- To see your changes, click OK at the bottom of the window.

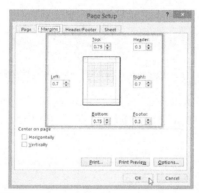

The margins of the notepad will be resized.

To include Print Titles:

Make sure the title headings are included on each page of your worksheet. The title headings appearing on the first page of a printed workbook would be confusing. Print Titles instructions let you choose which rows and columns appear on each page.

- Page Layout ➔ Print Layout ➔ Print Titles.

You may now make modifications to your page via Page Setup. Each page may have the same rows and columns from here on out. In our situation, a row will be repeated.

Next, pick the Collapse Dialogs option to see rows to repeat at the top.

The page Setup dialogue box is collapsed, and the mouse cursor is replaced with a selection arrow. Select the rows you want to repeat so that each printed page has the same row. Let's look at the first row.

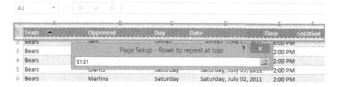

Row one will be inserted into the Rows for repeating at the top field. The "Collapse Dialog" should be reactivated.

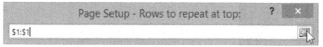

The Page Setup dialogue box may be enlarged by clicking on the arrows. To confirm your decision, press the OK button. Row 1 will be on top of every page.

To insert a page break:

Adding a page break to your worksheet lets you print different portions. Page breaks are vertical and horizontal. Page breaks divide columns and rows. Here's a horizontal page split.

Here is the Page Break command. It's in Page Break mode.

Choose the check box below where you want the page break to appear. After row 28, pick a page break (in this case, 29).

Click Page Layout on the Ribbon and pick Breaks.

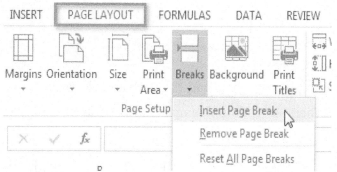

Place the dark blue page break bar.

	A	B	C	D	E	F
19	Bulls	Lightning	Saturday	Saturday, June 18, 2011	10:00 AM	
20	Cavaliers	Eagles	Friday	Friday, August 05, 2011	6:00 PM	
21	Cavaliers	Hawks	Friday	Friday, June 17, 2011	6:00 PM	
22	Cavaliers	Bears	Saturday	Saturday, August 13, 2011	2:00 PM	
23	Cavaliers	Bulls	Saturday	Saturday, June 25, 2011	2:00 PM	
24	Cavaliers	Lightning	Saturday	Saturday, July 16, 2011	2:00 PM	
25	Cavaliers	Tigers	Saturday	Saturday, July 02, 2011	2:00 PM	
26	Cavaliers	Colts	Saturday	Saturday, August 20, 2011	10:00 AM	
27	Cavaliers	Giants	Saturday	Saturday, July 23, 2011	10:00 AM	
28	Cavaliers	Jets	Saturday	Saturday, July 09, 2011	10:00 AM	
29	Colts	Lightning	Friday	Friday, July 01, 2011	6:00 PM	
30	Colts	Bears	Saturday	Saturday, June 25, 2011	2:00 PM	
31	Colts	Eagles	Saturday	Saturday, August 13, 2011	2:00 PM	
32	Colts	Hawks	Saturday	Saturday, July 30, 2011	2:00 PM	
33	Colts	Jets	Saturday	Saturday, July 23, 2011	2:00 PM	
34	Colts	Marlins	Saturday	Saturday, June 18, 2011	2:00 PM	
35	Colts	Cavaliers	Saturday	Saturday, August 20, 2011	10:00 AM	

Solid grey lines represent extra page breaks, whereas dashed grey lines indicate automatic page breaks in Normal mode.

To insert headers and footers:

Headers & footers improve worksheet readability and presentation. The worksheet's header and footer are shown in the top and bottom margins. Headers and footers often include page numbers, dates, and workbook names.

The Page Layout command is near the bottom of Excel. Page Layout mode displays the worksheet.

Choose a new header or footer. This page's footer will change.

- Your Ribbon will display a new tab titled Header & Footer Tools. Commands that contain dates, page numbers, & workbook names may be found here. Page numbers will be added to this sample.

- The page numbers will be added to the footer automatically.

2.2 ADDING NEW ROWS AND COLUMNS

Organize your spreadsheet by adding and deleting columns and rows.

Inserting or deleting a column

Use the Home Insert (Sheet Columns) option to add or remove sheet columns.

Alternatively, by clicking the column's header, you may pick Insert or Delete from the context menu.

Inserting or deleting a row

If you want to add or remove sheet rows, you may select a cell in the row and then go to Home ➔ Insert ➔ Add or Remove Sheet Rows.

Alternatively, you may pick Insert or Delete from the context menu by right-clicking on the row number.

Formatting options

When you enter a new column or row after selecting one with formatting, the formatting is copied. If you do not want to format, choose Insert Options after inserting and pick one of these options:

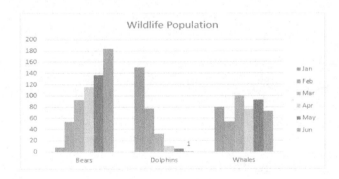

If the Add Options button is still not visible, click on File ➔ Options ➔ Advanced and check the Cut, copy, and paste group.

Creating charts

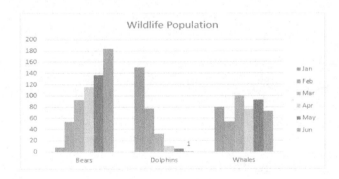

2.3 CONDITIONAL FORMATTING & DATA FILTERS

Conditional formatting using Excel highlights cells based on their value.

Highlighting Cells Rules

To highlight cells greater than a value, execute the following steps.

1. Select the range A1: A10

	A	B
1	14	
2	6	
3	39	
4	43	
5	2	
6	95	
7	5	
8	11	
9	86	
10	57	
11		

2. Click the Conditional Formatting within the Styles category on the home tab.

		Normal	Bad	Good	Neutral
Conditional Formatting ▾	Format as Table ▾	Calculation	Check Cell	Explanatory ...	Input

Styles

3. Then, choose Greater Than from the Cells Rules menu.

Highlight Cells Rules ▸	Greater Than...	
Top/Bottom Rules ▸	Less Than...	
Data Bars ▸	Between...	
Color Scales ▸	Equal To...	
Icon Sets ▸	Text that Contains...	
New Rule...	A Date Occurring...	
Clear Rules ▸	Duplicate Values...	
Manage Rules...	More Rules...	

4. Enter that value and choose a style to format the number 80.

Greater Than	? ×
Format cells that are GREATER THAN:	
80	with Light Red Fill with Dark Red Text ∨
	OK Cancel

Select "OK."

5. Result. Cells that are bigger than 80 are marked as such in Excel.

	A	B
1	14	
2	6	
3	39	
4	43	
5	2	
6	95	
7	5	
8	11	
9	86	
10	57	
11		

6. Change cell A1's value to 81.

Excel has automatically changed cell A1's format.

	A	B
1	81	
2	6	
3	39	
4	43	
5	2	
6	95	
7	5	
8	11	
9	86	
10	57	
11		

Clear Rules

Execute the following procedures to remove a conditional formatting rule.

The A1: A10 range should be selected.

2. Click on Conditional Formatting within the Styles category on your home tab.

You may also clear the rules from your selected cells by clicking Clear Rules.

Top/Bottom

Follow these procedures to draw attention to particularly noteworthy cells.

The A1: A10 range should be selected.

2. Click on the Conditional Formatting within the Styles category on your home tab.

3. Select Above Average, Top/Bottom Rules.

4. Select your formatting style.

5. Press OK.

Result. Excel calculates the average (42.5), and the cells over this average are formatted.

Conditional Formatting using Formulas

To enhance your Excel skills, use a formula to determine which cells should be formatted. Formulas of Conditional formatting must respond to FALSE & TRUE.

Choose the A 1: E 5 range.

	A	B	C	D	E	F
1	90	77	33	20	96	
2	59	66	20	61	44	
3	94	99	97	41	52	
4	36	43	70	13	54	
5	15	6	28	28	15	
6						

On your home tab, go to the Styles section and choose Conditional Formatting.

Select "New Rule."

To choose which cells for formatting, click on "Use a formula."
Now Type = ISODD into the formula (A 1)

Then Click on OK after selecting one formatting option.

Result. Each odd number is highlighted in Excel.

	A	B	C	D	E	F
1	90	77	33	20	96	
2	59	66	20	61	44	
3	94	99	97	41	52	
4	36	43	70	13	54	
5	15	6	28	28	15	
6						

Explanation: Always write your formula for the upper-left cell in the specified range. The formula is automatically copied to the other cells by Excel. As a consequence, cell A2 has the formula = ISODD (A2), & the same holds for the cs A 3 forward.

Here's another illustration.

Choose the A2: D7 range.

	A	B	C	D	E
1	Last Name	Sales	Country	Quarter	
2	Smith	$16,753.00	UK	Qtr 3	
3	Johnson	$14,808.00	USA	Qtr 4	
4	Williams	$10,644.00	UK	Qtr 2	
5	Jones	$1,390.00	USA	Qtr 3	
6	Brown	$4,865.00	USA	Qtr 4	
7	Williams	$12,438.00	UK	Qtr 1	
8					

Follow steps 2-4 again.
Type =$C2="USA" in the formula box.

After choosing a formatting option, click OK.

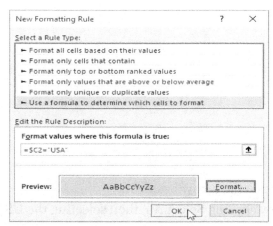

Result. Excel shows all USA orders in bold.

	A	B	C	D	E
1	Last Name	Sales	Country	Quarter	
2	Smith	$16,753.00	UK	Qtr 3	
3	Johnson	$14,808.00	USA	Qtr 4	
4	Williams	$10,644.00	UK	Qtr 2	
5	Jones	$1,390.00	USA	Qtr 3	
6	Brown	$4,865.00	USA	Qtr 4	
7	Williams	$12,438.00	UK	Qtr 1	
8					

Adding a $ sign in front of a column letter ($C2) corrected the reference to column C. Consequently, the formula =$C2="USA" is also present in cells B 2, C 2, and D 2, as well as cells A 3, B 3, C 3, and D3.

Data filter

Use Excel filtering to see entries that fulfill a certain set of conditions.
A data set may be accessed by selecting a single cell and clicking on it.
Select Filter from the Filter & Sort group on your Data tab.

The column headings have arrows in them.

	A	B	C	D	E
1	Last Nan ▼	Sales ▼	Count ▼	Quart ▼	
2	Smith	$16,753.00	UK	Qtr 3	
3	Johnson	$14,808.00	USA	Qtr 4	
4	Williams	$10,644.00	UK	Qtr 2	
5	Jones	$1,390.00	USA	Qtr 3	
6	Brown	$4,865.00	USA	Qtr 4	
7	Williams	$12,438.00	UK	Qtr 1	
8	Johnson	$9,339.00	UK	Qtr 2	
9	Smith	$18,919.00	USA	Qtr 3	
10	Jones	$9,213.00	USA	Qtr 4	
11	Jones	$7,433.00	UK	Qtr 1	
12	Brown	$3,255.00	USA	Qtr 2	
13	Williams	$14,867.00	USA	Qtr 3	
14	Williams	$19,302.00	UK	Qtr 4	
15	Smith	$9,698.00	USA	Qtr 1	
16					

Select your country by clicking the arrow beside it.

Clear all your checkboxes by clicking Select All, then selecting the USA from the drop-down menu.

Select "OK."

Result. Excel only shows data from the United States.

	A	B	C	D	E
1	Last Nan ▼	Sales ▼	Count ▼	Quart ▼	
3	Johnson	$14,808.00	USA	Qtr 4	
5	Jones	$1,390.00	USA	Qtr 3	
6	Brown	$4,865.00	USA	Qtr 4	
9	Smith	$18,919.00	USA	Qtr 3	
10	Jones	$9,213.00	USA	Qtr 4	
12	Brown	$3,255.00	USA	Qtr 2	
13	Williams	$14,867.00	USA	Qtr 3	
15	Smith	$9,698.00	USA	Qtr 1	
16					

Click on the arrow beside Quarter to bring up the context menu.

When you're done, click Select All to remove all the checkboxes, then select the checkbox beside Qtr 4.

Click the OK button.

Results. Excel only displays sales within the United States into the fourth quarter.

	A	B	C	D	E
1	Last Nan ▾	Sales ▾	Count ▾	Quart ▾	
3	Johnson	$14,808.00	USA	Qtr 4	
6	Brown	$4,865.00	USA	Qtr 4	
10	Jones	$9,213.00	USA	Qtr 4	
16					

Click Clear within Sort & Filter on your Data tab to remove the filter. To remove the arrows and the filter, click Filter.

Excel data may be more quickly filtered.

Select the cell in the table by clicking on it.

	A	B	C	D	E
1	Last Name	Sales	Country	Quarter	
2	Smith	$16,753.00	UK	Qtr 3	
3	Johnson	$14,808.00	USA	Qtr 4	
4	Williams	$10,644.00	UK	Qtr 2	
5	Jones	$1,390.00	USA	Qtr 3	
6	Brown	$4,865.00	USA	Qtr 4	
7	Williams	$12,438.00	UK	Qtr 1	
8	Johnson	$9,339.00	UK	Qtr 2	
9	Smith	$18,919.00	USA	Qtr 3	
10	Jones	$9,213.00	USA	Qtr 4	
11	Jones	$7,433.00	UK	Qtr 1	
12	Brown	$3,255.00	USA	Qtr 2	
13	Williams	$14,867.00	USA	Qtr 3	
14	Williams	$19,302.00	UK	Qtr 4	
15	Smith	$9,698.00	USA	Qtr 1	
16					

Then, right-click and choose Filter, select Filter the Selected Cell's Value, and click OK.

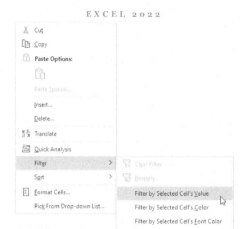

Result. Excel shows data from the United States.

	A	B	C	D	E
1	Last Nan ▾	Sales ▾	Count ▾	Quart ▾	
3	Johnson	$14,808.00	USA	Qtr 4	
5	Jones	$1,390.00	USA	Qtr 3	
6	Brown	$4,865.00	USA	Qtr 4	
9	Smith	$18,919.00	USA	Qtr 3	
10	Jones	$9,213.00	USA	Qtr 4	
12	Brown	$3,255.00	USA	Qtr 2	
13	Williams	$14,867.00	USA	Qtr 3	
15	Smith	$9,698.00	USA	Qtr 1	
16					

Cursor & Dragging

A Fill Handle is a strong Excel autofill feature in the current cell's bottom right corner. It copies values down the column or fills a string of numbers, dates, messages, formulae, or a similar sequence to a specified number of cells. The mouse cursor transforms from the white cross towards the black plus sign over the fill handle. Click & hold your handle to move between cells. When you remove the mouse button, all dragged cells are auto-filled.

Fill handle saves time and prevents human error (like typos).

Using the AutoFill with Excel

Excel's autofill function is accessible through the fill handle. It's like copy-and-paste, but much more. Fill handle isn't the only technique to utilize autofill.

First, choose a cell's range, beginning with the cell holding the data to be duplicated. Ctrl+D to copy, Ctrl+R to fill right.

Fill Button - Click the 'Fill' button within the Editing category of the 'Home' tab to get the fill command. Down, Up, Left, Right, Series, Justify, Across Worksheets, & Flash Fill is available.

Double-click the Fill handle to autofill a column. Double-click the fill handle to swiftly fill down the column if the next cell has data. If your data collection contains blank cells, this will fill in an adjacent blank cell.

Duplicate Data with Fill Handle

The fill handle copies cell content to multiple cells. Using the fill handle, you may effortlessly copy text, numbers, formulae, etc.

Simply choose the cell(s) you wish to copy & drag the fill handle in either direction. It rapidly fills dragged-over cells with specified cell data.

Double-clicking on your fill handle in cell C2 will fill this column till C9 since data is in B9.

Autofill Options

When you drag a fill handle, it identifies data patterns & fills your list while giving you choices.

After dragging your fill handle (or double-clicking) and filling the list, the 'Auto Fill Options' icon appears in the bottom right corner.

Depending on the data, clicking this symbol gives you the following options:

- **Copy cells** – This will duplicate the first cell throughout the list of cells you've chosen.

- **Fill series** – Fill the chosen cells with a sequence or set of values, starting with the original cell value, using the option

- **Fill formatting** – However, this one does not include any data in the given range.

- **Filling Without formatting** – Fills the chosen range with the beginning cell's data, but not with the formatting

- **Flash fill** – This option uses data patterns to populate a list of items. As an illustration, the Flash fill feature inside the example below fills in the list by identifying 2000 as 20%, assuming 3000 as 30%, and assuming 6500 as 65%.

Agent	Sales	Commission
Ben	2000	20%
Rick	3000	30%
James	6500	65%
Van	1200	12%
Nick	6522	65%
Pen	3120	31%
Wen	3200	32%
Wyett	2800	28%

○ Copy Cells
○ Fill Series
○ Fill Formatting Only
○ Fill Without Formatting
◉ Flash Fill

Autofill Text Value with Fill Handle

Excel fill handle autocompletes a list by duplicating the starting cell's text contents (s). It can also identify day names, month names, & other text sequences. Abbreviated or complete names of months, weekdays, etc.

First, put month abbreviations or complete names in the first field, then utilize your fill handle for filling additional cells.

Weekdays

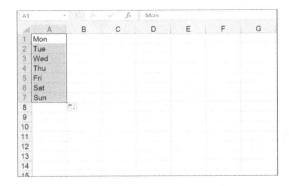

The fill handle may also autocomplete number-based text. First, type text in one cell, then use the fill handle to fill others.

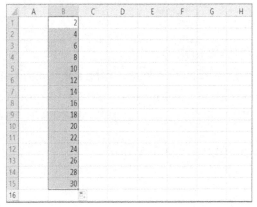

Autofill Numbers with Fill Handle

The fill handle creates a number sequence. It might be odd, even, or 1-increment numbers, etc.

Select almost 2 numbers to create a pattern for the first two cells, then drag the fill handle.

Excel copies the same number if you pick one cell containing a number & drag it down since there isn't any pattern inside one number.

Enter "2" in B1 and "4" in B2. Select B1 and B2 and slide the AutoFill handle lower to get even numbers.

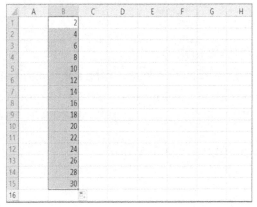

When you choose 'Auto Fill Choices,' the following options appear:

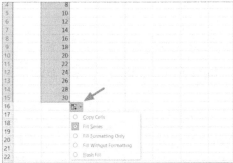

Instead of dragging with the left mouse button, use the right mouse button. When you release it, other alternatives will appear, as seen below.

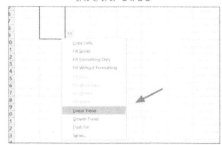

You've covered the first four & flash-fill possibilities; now, let's look at the others.

Linear Trend options – Excel makes a straight-line chart with linear numbers.

Growth Trend options – Excel uses the initial data to calculate an exponential growth series.

Series option – This opens the Series dialogue with advanced settings.

Copying Formulas with Fill Handles

It is like copying numbers along a column or auto-fill a succession of values when you copy a formula.

Drag your fill handle from one cell to another to duplicate the formula in those other cells. Whenever you copy a formula, it will immediately update to reflect the new location of the cell where you pasted it.

Using the fill handle, copy the formula from cell B1 to B10.

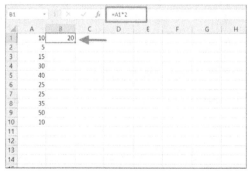

When a cell is next to another, the formula automatically adapts.

You'll get results for all the rows.

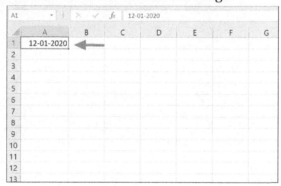

Autofill Dates with Fill Handle

Enter your dates within the first cell of a range in either format, which Excel recognizes to automatically fill within dates in the rest of the cells in the range.

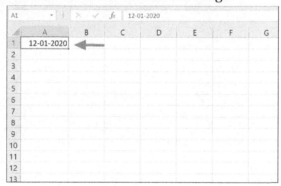

Drag your fill handle downwards to a cell where you'd like the date to finish, and then release it to release the date.

For dates, extra AutoFill choices appear when you select the "Auto Fill Options" icon just at the end of an auto-filled range, as shown in the following illustration.

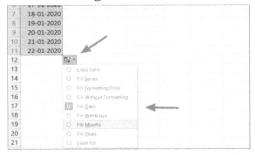

Along with the five pre-existing choices, you'll find four more advanced date selections in this section:

Fill Days – This adds one more day to the list by incrementing the value by one.

Fill Weekdays – Only weekdays are included in the lists, eliminating Saturdays and Sundays.

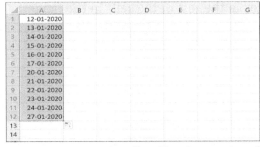

Fill Months – While the day stays constant in all cells, the option fills your list with months that increase sequentially.

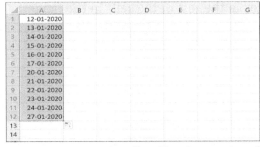

Fill Years – These years are added one at a time while day & month stay static.

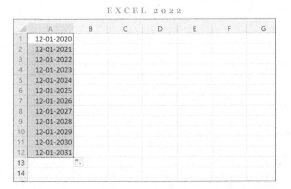

2.4 CREATING THE CUSTOM LISTS FOR YOUR AUTOFILLING DATA

Lists don't always have to be organized in the same manner. You can use Excel's built-in lists to arrange data in these situations. Fill handles may be used to populate cells from the custom list.
Select 'File' from the menu and then 'Options'.

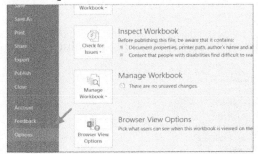

The "Edit Custom Lists." button may be found under the "General" section within the right pane by selecting "Advanced" within the left panel.
To go to the Custom List dialogue box, click on the button.

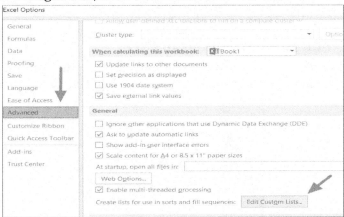

Right-clicking on "Advanced" in the left-hand panel brings up a menu containing the "Edit Custom Lists." button. To access your Custom Lists dialogue, click the button.

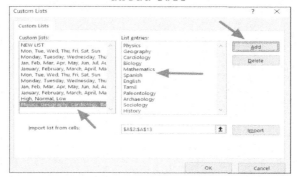

Select the cell where you want your list and enter the 1st item of the custom list, then save your list.

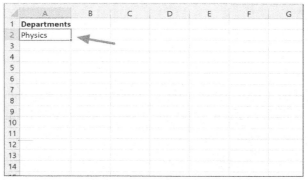

Once you've dragged the fill handle, the custom list of values will be used to auto-fill the cells.

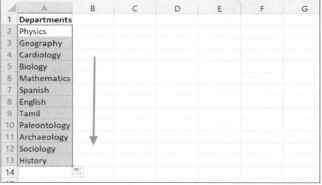

Disable or Enable your AutoFill Options in Excel

In Excel, if your fill handle isn't functioning, you may activate the Autofill functionality on the Excel options: Other options may be found by clicking on the "File" tab & then selecting "Options".

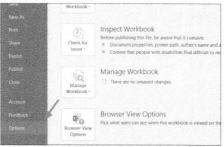

Activate the fill handle & cell drag and drop by selecting 'Advanced' in Excel & checking the 'Editing Options' option. This will allow Excel's fill handle.

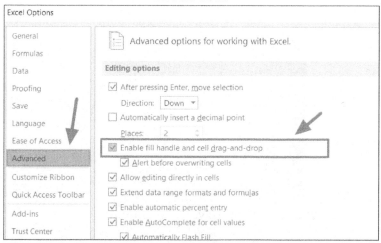

Then click on 'OK' to exit this dialogue box, and you're done.

2.5 IMPORT / EXPORT DATA

In addition to the standard.xslx format, Excel can export and import various other file formats. A separate file type may be required if your saving data will be shared with other applications, such as a database.

Export Data

A CSV or a text file may be used to move data from Excel to different software, such as another spreadsheet application.

Go to the Files tabs.

Click the Export from your menu on the left.

Click your Change File Format button.

To pick a file type, click on Other File Types.

Text (Tab delimited): A tab will be used to separate every cell data.

CSV (Comma delimited): A comma will be used to denote the end of each row of information in the table.

Formatted Texts (space delimited): A space will be used to separate the data in each cell.

Save as some other File Type: When you Save As dialogue box pops up, choose a new file type.

The file you choose will depend on the software that will use the exported data.

Click on Save As.

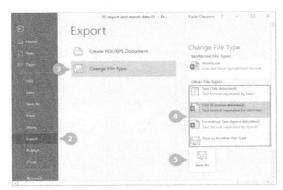

Select some location where you want to store your document.

Save your work.

You'll see a warning that a portion of the workbook's functionality will be lost when you do this.

Click on Yes.

Import Data

External data sources, such as other databases, files, & web pages, may be imported into Excel.

- On the Ribbon, choose the Data tab.

- The Get Data button may be accessed by clicking on it.

Certain data sources need specific security access, & the connecting procedure might be complicated. For assistance, contact the technical support team at your company.

- Select a File from the drop-down menu.

- Select from CSV/Text.

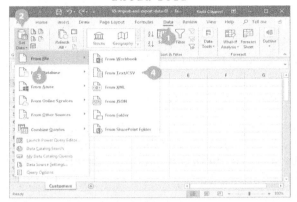

To import data from an external source, pick one of the Get External Data choices within Get the External Data groups instead.

Import the file you desire by clicking on the file's name.

Import your file by clicking on the Import button.

If a security warning displays when importing external data stating that a connection to an external source may not be secure, click OK.

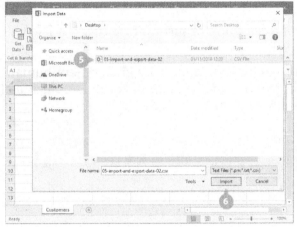

Make sure the preview is accurate.

The delimiter has been defined since you indicated that commas split the data. This option allows you to make any necessary adjustments.

Click on Load.

CHAPTER 3: ADVANCED FEATURES OF EXCEL

Learners must know Excel formulae before doing financial research. Microsoft Excel is a standard data-processing program. Microsoft's spreadsheet tool is popular among investment bankers and financial analysts for data analysis, modeling, and presentation. This book contains an overview and collection of Excel functions.

3.1 BASIC TERMS IN EXCEL

In Excel, formulas and functions are used for computations.

1. Formulas
Excel formulas operate for a cell count or just a single cell. = A 1 + A 2 + A 3 finds A1-A3 values.

2. Functions
Functions in Excel are pre-defined formulae. By giving them human-friendly names, they do away with the time-consuming manual involvement of formulae. Such as (A1:A3) = SUM. The function totals the values from A1 through A3.

3.2 FIVE TIME-SAVING EXCEL DATA INSERTION METHODS

There are five distinct methods for using basic Excel formulae when examining the outcomes. Every strategy offers a unique set of advantages. Therefore, let's go over those tactics before discussing the important formulae so that you may begin working on your preferred procedure immediately.

1. Simple insertion: Typing the formula in a cell
Simple Excel formulae may be inserted by putting a single formula into the cells or utilizing the formula bar. The Excel feature name is usually followed by one equal sign at the start of the operation.

Excel is ingenious because a pop-up feature hint appears when you write the function phrase. From this selection, you will choose your choice. But refrain from pressing the Enter key. Instead, use the Tab key to start adding more options. Otherwise, you can get an incorrect name error that appears as "#NAME?" Simply pick that cell and finish the role in your formula bar to fix it.

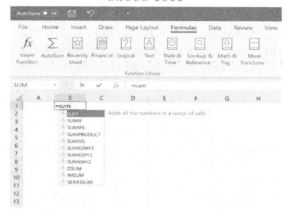

2. Using the Insert Function Options from your Formulas Tab

You need an Excel Insert Feature dialogue box to fully use the function insertion's potential. To accomplish this, choose Insert Function from the first option on your Formula tab. You may find many of the responsibilities you'll need in your conversation box to complete the financial report.

3. Selecting the Formula among the Groups from Formula Tab

This option is for those who like quick access to their favorite features. To reach that menu, choose the Formulas tab and your preferred category. Click to see a sub-menu with a list of these features. Then, you may make your chosen selection. If your preferred category isn't shown on the page, go to More Functions and check; it's hidden there.

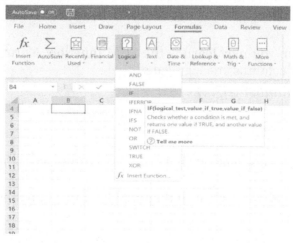

4. Using an AutoSum Option

For routine and easy chores, AutoSum is the preferred choice. Therefore, choose the home tab and click the AutoSum button in the upper-right corner. Then click the caret to bring up any previously concealed formulae. This option is also available in your Formulas tab following the Insert Function.

5. Quick Insert: Using Recently Utilized Tabs

If inputting the most often used formula again seems laborious, try using the Currently Used option instead. It is the third menu option under AutoSum on the Formulas tab.

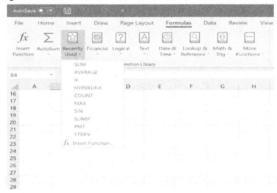

3.3 SEVEN EXCEL FORMULAS FOR THE WORKFLOW

Since you can now input and apply your favorite formulae properly, let's start by looking at some fundamental Excel functions.

1. SUM

The first Excel calculation you may learn is the SUM function. Normally, values from the specified settings' selected rows or columns are aggregated.

= *SUM (**number 1**, [number 2], ...)*

Examples:

= *SUM (B 2: G 2)* – A basic selection that sums all values of a single row.

= *SUM (A 2: A 8)* – A basic selection that sums all values of a single column.

= *SUM (A 2: A 7, A 9, A 12: A 15)* – A complex collection which sums values of range A2-A7, skips A 8, adds A 9, jumps A 10 & A 11, then ultimateladdsdd from A 12-A 15.

= *SUM (A 2: A 8) / 20* – Demonstrates you can turn the function into a formula.

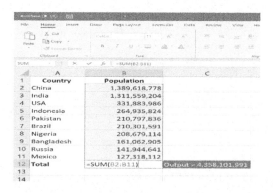

2. Average
Simple averages of the results should be considered while utilizing the AVERAGE function, much like the total number of owners within the given shareholding pool.

= *AVERAGE (**number 1**, [number 2], …)*

Example:

= *AVERAGE (B 2: B 11)* – Demonstrates an average and alike (SUM (B 2: B 11) / 10)

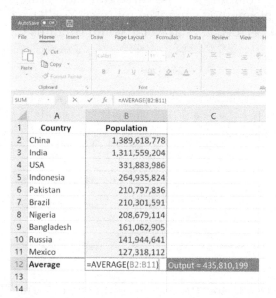

3. Count
A collection of cells with solely numerical values is counted using the COUNT feature.

= *COUNT (**value 1**, **[value 2]**, …)*

Example:

COUNT (A: A) – enters a total for all numerical values in column A. To count rows, however, you need to change a range in the calculation.

COUNT (A 1: C 1) – Now, it could count the rows.

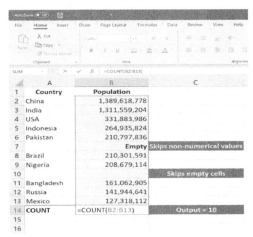

4. COUNTY

All cells within a rage are counted using COUNTA's COUNT feature, for example. However, regardless of cell type, it does count all cells. Unlike COUNT, which exclusively saves numeric data, it often counts dates, days, sequences, logical values, errors, void strings, and text.

*=COUNTA (***value 1, [value 2], ...***)*

Example:

COUNTA (C 2: C 13) - The C column's rows 2 through 13 are tallied regardless of the sort. However, unlike COUNT, a comparable method cannot count rows. You'll need to change the range between the brackets; for example, COUNTA (C 2: H 2) would count columns in the C and H categories.

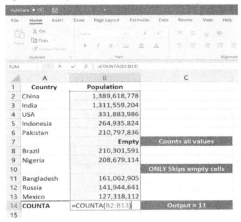

5. IF

This function may also be used to sort the data according to criteria. The IF formula's advantage is that it enables the usage of formulae and functions.

*=IF (***logical test, [value_if_false] [value_if_true],***)*

Example:

=IF (C 2<D 3, 'TRUE,' 'FALSE') – It determines if C 3 is lower than D 3 in terms of value. Your cell value should stay TRUE if your reasoning is correct or false.

=IF (SUM (C 1: C 10)➔SUM (D 1: D 10), SUM (C 1: C 10), SUM (D 1: D 10)) – IF logic situation that is challenging. It initially adds up C 1–C10 and D 1–D10 before comparing the numbers. A cell's value becomes equal to a sum of C 1-C10 when the total of C1-C10 surpasses the sum of D 1-D10. Otherwise, it is the sum of C1 through C10.

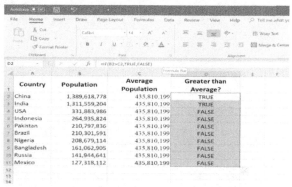

6. The TRIM

Thanks to the TRIM function, unruly spaces won't lead to problems in your routines. It denotes the absence of open places. TRIM only affects a single cell, unlike many other activities that could affect a group of cells. Its disadvantage is that it duplicates information in a spreadsheet.

*=TRIM (***text***)*

Example:

TRIM (A 2) – Deletes any empty spaces from the values in cell A-2.

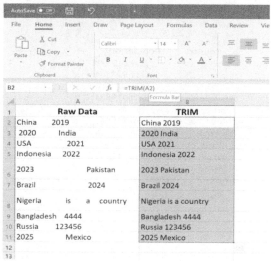

7. MAX and MIN

Finding the highest and lowest values within a group of data is made easier with the help of the MAX and MIN functions.

*=MIN (***number 1***, [number 2], ...)*

Example:

=*MIN (B 2: C 11)* – The minimal number is determined between the B column from B 2 and C column from C 2 to 11 in all columns, B & C.

=*MAX (**number 1**, [number 2], ...)*

Example:

=*MAX (B 2: C 11)* – The greatest number among B column from B 2 and C column from C 2 to 11 row is considered for both columns B & C.

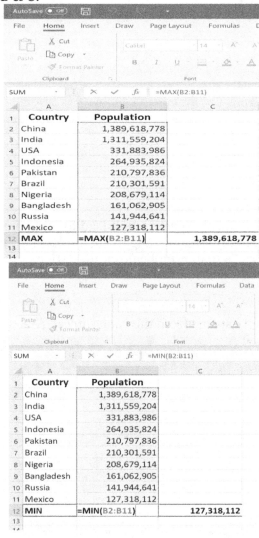

3.4 ADVANCED FORMULAS IN EXCEL

You have practiced some basic Excel formulas; Let's get into some advanced formulas in Excel.

WORKDAY.INTL FUNCTION

Use WORKDAY.INTL to estimate a project's completion date.

It's more flexible than WORKDAY, which assumed weekends were always Sunday and Saturday. You may pick different weekends or construct your list.

WORKDAY.INTL Arguments

WORKDAY.INTL requires 2 parameters and allows 2 more.

- **start_date:** the date on which the computation begins

- **days:** beginning and ending dates are counted as complete days

- **weekend: (optional)** working days are indicated with a special code

- **holidays: (optional)** calendar days that are not in use

Notes regarding WORKDAY.INTL

The WORKDAY.INTL function may be used in a variety of ways:

Start Date

- The first digit of the current date will be omitted, leaving just the integer

- A time and date, for example, will be disregarded if entered.

- For best results, choose a day that falls on a workday.

Days

We're going to round down the number of days to the nearest integer.

A number might be positive, negative, or zero to indicate forward or backward movement. A zero indicates a return to the beginning date.

Weekend

In this case, it's not required. Non-working days are Sunday and Saturday if they are not included.

To begin, let's have a look at this issue:

- Choose a choice from the drop-down menu

- A 7-digit array with one non-functional character and zero functioning characters may also be created.

Holidays

- In this case, it's not required. There are no specific non-working days if calendar dates are excluded.

Project End Date

The WORKDAY.INTL function may be used to compute the end date of a project in this example. Like WORKDAY, but with the ability to choose the days off.

As an example:

- Begin with the WORKDAY arguments. Start date & days for INTL.

- Then comes the Christmas shopping.

- Finally, non-working days would be designated.

Start with Basics

Two pieces of information are necessary to get started with WORKDAY.INTL function's basic features:

How long will it take to complete the task?

Now it's WORKDAY!

INTL will figure out when the required amount of time has passed from the start date to arrive at the actual working date.

You begin on Thursday, Dec 10th (cell C 8), and your project will be completed in two days, as shown in the screenshot (cell C10).

Cell C12 has the following WORKDAY.INTL formula:

=WORKDAY.INTL (C8, C10)

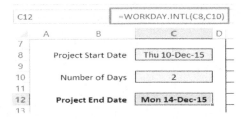

Check your Calculation

See the following table to see why December 14th was chosen.

Thursdays and Fridays are dedicated to working on the project (2 days).

It thinks you don't work on Saturdays or Sundays since you didn't indicate them.

The following working day was Monday, Dec 14th; that is the formula's outcome.

Date	Work?	Project Day
Thu 10-Dec-15	1	1
Fri 11-Dec-15	1	2
Sat 12-Dec-15	0	
Sun 13-Dec-15	0	
Mon 14-Dec-15	1	
Tue 15-Dec-15	1	

Adjust your End Date

Instead of the following business day, you'd want to know when the job is expected to be done. So, you deduct one from the number of days within the calculation to get the desired result.

=WORKDAY.INTL (C8, C10-1)

That makes Friday, December 11, the end date for the project.

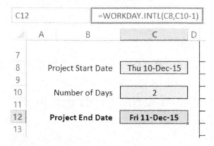

Exclude Holidays

Like the earlier WORKDAY function, you may omit holidays from WORKDAY.INTL.

Adding or removing dates is trivial in a named Excel table. In the image below, tblHol's date column is the Holiday List.

Enter a List of Holidays

Date	Holiday
26-Nov-2015	Thanksgiving
25-Dec-2015	Christmas
26-Dec-2015	Boxing Day
1-Jan-2016	New Year's Day

You'll use the function's fourth parameter to omit holidays from date computations.

=WORKDAY.INTL (C8,C10-1,tblHol[Date])

With this change, a project that started on December 24 will expire on December 28.

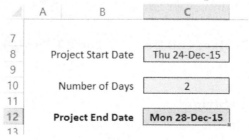

Here's a table containing working days and orange-highlighted holidays.

Date	Work?	Project Day
Thu 24-Dec-15	1	1
Fri 25-Dec-15	0	
Sat 26-Dec-15	0	
Sun 27-Dec-15	0	
Mon 28-Dec-15	**1**	2
Tue 29-Dec-15	1	

Specify your Non-Working Days

If you don't say, WORKDAY. INTL ignores weekends (non-working days) automatically. You may pick other days as weekends using either method:

- choose from the list

- 1 & 0 string

Select from the Drop-Down List

Selecting from a drop-down list of alternatives makes it much simpler to designate weekend days. The list will immediately display when you begin the function with the third parameter.

If you don't see the list, use Alt + Down Arrow to bring it up.

Option 2 - Sunday, Monday – shifts the project deadline to Tuesday, Dec 29th.

=WORKDAY.INTL(C8, C101,2, tblHol[Da)

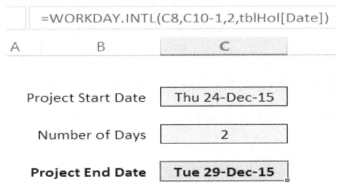

Create Non-Working Days String

Create your string if none of the drop-down selections are what you're looking for.

Weekdays are represented by the first seven numbers of the string.

- Workdays are marked with a zero.

- For non-working days, use a 1.

Just use string 0101011 if you just work on Mondays, Wednesdays, and Fridays.

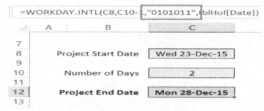

You'll modify the start date to Wednesday, December 23rd, a working day in our new calendar. Below is the amended formula with a 7-digit string within double quotation marks in the third parameter.

=WORKDAY.INTL (C8,C10-1,"0101011",tblHol[Date])

As a result of these modifications, the deadline has been moved forward to Monday, Dec 28th.

Calculate Non-Working String

A table like the one below might make it simpler to pick non-working days. Use an X to indicate days off from work and an IF formula that displays 0 or 1 in every row.

=IF (K8="x",1,0)

A CONCATENATE formula is used to condense the string into its final form:

= CONCATENATE (M8, M9, M10, M11, M12, M13, M14)

Use that cell as the 3rd parameter within WORKDAY.INTL calculation.

=WORKDAY.INTL (C 8, C 10-1, M 15, tblHol [Date])

Your calculation columns might be concealed to prevent individuals from mucking up formulae.

Nth Weekdays of the Month (WORKDAY.INTL)

The DAY AT WORK. Using the INTL function along with one customized string of the nonworking days, one may get the Nth weekday of the month.

Excel's WORKDAY.INTL function may be utilized to discover the Nth weekday into a given month and year. Thanksgiving in Canada is honored on the 2nd Monday in Oct, so check the calendar to see when it falls this year.

Examples: Thanksgiving Day USA - Nth Weekday of the Month

In the United States, for example, Thanksgiving falls on the fourth Thursday of November.

The following formula, seen in cell C10 of the image below, may be used to determine the date of Thanksgiving:

=WORKDAY.INTL (DATE (C4, D5, 0), C7, "1110111")

There is one working day (Thursday) within a 7-digit string for non-working days.

Because of this, the actual Thanksgiving date is the fourth Thursday of November.

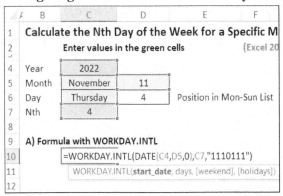

THE RANDBETWEEN FUNCTION

Based on the input values, the RANDBETWEEN function outputs a random number. Every time the worksheet is accessed or edited, this feature is activated.

The following parameters are used when using the RANDBETWEEN function:

Down: This is the least integer in the set that the function may return (Mandatory Function).

Peak The greatest integer the function may produce in the set (Mandatory Function).

Application of RANDBETWEEN Function

Let's examine the table below to see how the RANDBETWEEN function is used.

	f_x	=RANDBETWEEN(A2, B2)	

	A	B	C	D
	Bottom	Top	Result	
2	2	3	3	
3	3	10	4	
4	120	300	205	
5	32	121	102	

The table above uses the RANDBETWEEN method (A2, B2).

The worksheet's outcome varies when the equations in the table are repeated, as seen below.

	A	B	C	D
1	Bottom	Top	Result	
2	2	3	2	
3	3	10	8	
4	120	300	181	
5	32	121	87	

fx =RANDBETWEEN(A2, B2)

RANDBETWEEN has a few considerations.

When tabulated or changed, RANDBETWEEN returns a new value.

Enter the RANDBETWEEN function in the formula bar and press F9 to change the model into its output. Choose a cell, enter RANDBETWEEN, then press Ctrl + Enter.

TRANSPOSE FUNCTION

TRANSPOSE flips a spectrum or array. Vertical and horizontal ranges are transformed.
TRANSPOSE has one parameter. =Transpose (array)
Select blank cells. Ensure the chosen cells' numbers match the original set.

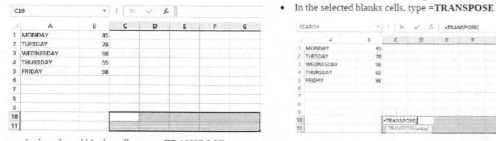

- In the selected blanks cells, type =TRANSPOSE

Transpose cells in their native environment.

CTRL+SHIF+ENTER transposes the cell range.

COUNTBLANK FUNCTION

Excel's STATISTICAL functions include COUNTBLANK[1]. COUNTBLANK counts a range's empty cells.

The function may highlight or count empty cells in financial analysis.

Formula

=COUNTBLANK (range)

Where:

Range defines which cells to count as blank.

For COUNTBLANK:

- This function doesn't count text, numbers, mistakes, etc.

- Empty formulas ("") are counted. COUNTBLANK counts a cell as blank if it contains a blank text string and formula that yields one.

- Zero-filled cells aren't counted as blank.

Using COUNTBLANK Function within Excel?

COUNTBLANK can be used in a worksheet cell's formula. Consider an example to learn the function's applications.

COUNTBLANK Example

This method uses conditional formatting to count empty cells.

Consider the following data:

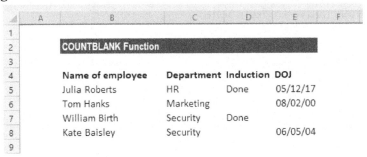

	A	B	C	D	E	F
1						
2		COUNTBLANK Function				
3						
4		Name of employee	Department	Induction	DOJ	
5		Julia Roberts	HR	Done	05/12/17	
6		Tom Hanks	Marketing		08/02/00	
7		William Birth	Security	Done		
8		Kate Baisley	Security		06/05/04	
9						

=COUNTBLANK (A2:D5) counts empty rows.

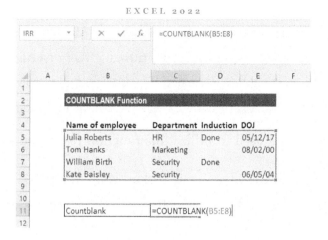

Results:

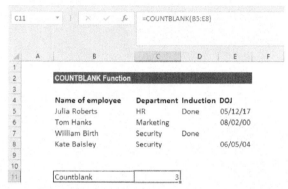

Using conditional formatting and COUNTBLANK, you may highlight rows containing empty cells. Select the required range, then apply COUNTBLANK() conditional formatting. This highlights all Blank cells in the range.

VLOOKUP FUNCTION

The VLOOKUP function looks up data within the 1st column of a dataset/table and returns equal data from a separate column in the same row.

VLOOKUP uses these parameters:

=VLOOKUP (col_index_num, table_array, lookup_value, [range_lookup])

- **Look-up_value (Required argument):** The value to look for in the table's or dataset's first column.

- **Table_array (Required argument):** the data array that the lookup value may search within the column's left-hand part.

- **Col_index_num (Needed argument):** The returned corresponding statistics are listed in the table as column numbers or integers.

- **Range_lookup (optional argument):** Whether VLOOK can discover an exact match or a good match depends on this piece of code. Either TRUE or FALSE determines the statement's value. The next highest value is returned if a suitable match cannot be found. FALSE indicates an exact match, and #N/A is returned as an error if none is discovered.

The steps listed below may be used to utilize this function to get the value of yam within the table above:

- Choose an empty cell, then type your lookup value method, that is, the cell containing the desired data. The lookup cell in this instance is A12, which has the formula Yam =VLOOKUP (A12)

HLOOKUP FUNCTION

The HLOOKUP function, which stands for "horizontal lookup," is a device for retrieving a value or a piece of information from the top row of a table array or dataset and returning it together with another row's given value or item in the same column.

The HLOOKUP function uses the following inputs to conduct its job.

(Lookup value, table array, row index number, [range lookup]) = HLOOKUP

Follow the instructions below to calculate your overall Joy in Mathematics score.

Select a blank cell, then enter the lookup value or the cell containing the data to be looked for.

- The lookup cell in this instance is B1, which contains the name. Pleasure; =HLOOKUP (B1

	A	B	C	D	E	F	G
1	STUDENT SCORES	JOY	LOVETH	JOHN	ADE X		
2	MATHEMATICS	59	45	68	98		
3	ENGLISH	69	78	43	76		
4	ECONOMICS	34	56	65	89		
5	PHE	23	89	24	97		
6							
7	THE TOTAL SCORE OF JOY IN MATHEMATICS	=HLOOKUP(B1					
8		HLOOKUP (lookup_value, table_array, row_index_num, [range_lookup])					

Finally, by selecting TRUE or FALSE, you may inform Excel whether you're looking for an exact or a great fit.

= HLOOKUP (B1, A1:E5,3, FALSE) or =HLOOKUP (B1, A1:E5, 3, TRUE)

X ✓ *fx* =HLOOKUP(B1, A1:E5,2, FALSE)

	A	B	C	D	E	F	G
1	STUDENT SCORES	JOY	LOVETH	JOHN	ADE X		
2	MATHEMATICS	59	45	68	98		
3	ENGLISH	69	78	43	76		
4	ECONOMICS	34	56	65	89		
5	PHE	23	89	24	97		
6							
7	THE TOTAL SCORE OF JOY IN MATHEMATICS	=HLOOKUP(B1, A1:E5,2, FALSE)					
8		HLOOKUP(lookup_value, table_array, row_index_num, [range_lookup])					

CHAPTER 4: EXCEL TABLES

This chapter covers Excel table fundamentals. This book creates a multi-sheet file for Jan. weather data in 2 cities. Most employees must organize, manage, and report outcomes.

This chapter's Figure shows a full workbook. This workbook contains three pages. The first worksheet depicts Portland, Maine's January weather. The 2nd page displays Jan's weather in Portland, Oregon, which is different. The third sheet adds a weekly column to Portland, Oregon results for subtotaling.

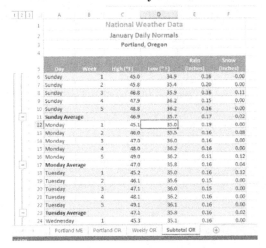

4.1 CREATING THE TABLE

A correctly set up table with a lengthy list or column helps present data. When entering data from scratch, follow these rules:

Use adjacent columns and rows to coordinate data.

Start your table at the top-left corner and proceed down.

Skipping rows and columns "spacings out" info. (Rows and columns may be enlarged and aligned to create white space between features.)

Set aside a column on the table's left for row headers.

Just above your table's rows, put the column titles.

Table titles should be placed above column heads in a row (s).

Following these recommendations will guarantee that the table's types, filters, totals, and subtotals provide desired results. You'll need these rules for a National Weather Portland M E worksheet. Now, your data is in rows and columns. The Upper left is now A5, and Row5 names are beneath column headers. After setting up your data, you're pleased to alter it in Excel. Open (CH5 Data) and save it as National Weather CH5.

A5 in Portland-ME.

On the Insert tab, click Table.

The figure appears onscreen.

Troublemaker
My table contains the headers" Okay.
Reload A5.
Adjust column widths to view row5 headers with filter arrows. Your table's filter arrows display as down-arrow buttons in row 5. You'll discover how to filter & sort data later in the chapter.
Your spreadsheet should resemble Figure.

	A	B	C	D	E
1		National Weather Data			
2		January Daily Normals			
3		Portland, Maine			
4					
5	Day	High (°F)	Low (° F)	Rain (Inches)	Snow (Inches)
6	1	32.5	15.1	0.12	0.59
7	2	32.3	14.8	0.12	0.59
8	3	32.1	14.6	0.11	0.73
9	4	31.9	14.4	0.08	0.49
10	5	31.8	14.2	0.12	0.71
11	6	31.6	14.0	0.12	0.59
12	7	31.4	13.9	0.12	0.59
13	8	31.3	13.7	0.12	0.59
14	9	31.2	13.6	0.07	0.63
15	10	31.1	3.4	0.12	0.67
16	11	31.0	13.3	0.12	0.63
17	12	30.9	13.2	0.12	0.71
18	13	30.8	13.1	0.12	0.67

Table Tool Design appears when you click within the table. This ribbon tab allows update, style, and application table features.
Follow these steps:

- Choose A5 or Portland.

- Insert tab, Table button.

- My table contains the headers" Okay.

- Reload A5.

- Adjust column widths to view row5 titles and filter arrows.

Creating the Table
- Select the top left cell in the data.

- Click the Table button under the Insert tab.

- The "My table contains headers" checkbox should be selected. Choose the OK option.

- Click once more on the top-left cell.

- Adjust the column widths to view all the headers with the filter arrows.

4.2 FORMATTING TABLES

There are several formatting options for the Excel table. Pre-installed table styles come in Light, Medium, and Dark color options. Below are also included many table designs.

Table Style Options

Table Style	Description
Header Row	Top row of the table that includes column headings
Total Row	Row added to the bottom that applies column summary calculations
First Column	Formatting added to the left-most column in the table
Last Column	Formatting added to the right-most column in the table
Banded Rows	Alternating rows of color added to make it easier to see rows of data
Banded Columns	Alternating columns of color added to make it easier to see columns of data
Filter Button	Button that appears at the top of each column that lists options for sorting and filtering

In the steps that follow, you'll format both of your Portland weather tables as follows:

1. Locate the Portland file in your open file (ME sheet).

2. On the Table Tool Design tab, click the Further button in the Table Style group.

A selection of table kinds will show up, as seen in the figure below.

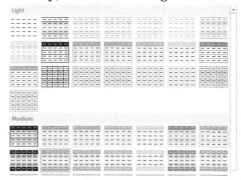

3. Select Table Styles Medium 7 from the Medium Section of the Table Style collection.

4. On the Ribbon, choose Banded Rows under the Table Styles Option category.

The color-contrasting line would disappear. Reading the data in the table has gotten more difficult.

5. Try out one of the many Table Styles options. Once finished, just choose the Banded Rows, Header Row, and Filter Button, as shown in the figure below.

☑ Header Row	☐ First Column	☑ Filter Button
☐ Total Row	☐ Last Column	
☑ Banded Rows	☐ Banded Columns	

Table Style Options

4.3 ADDING DATA TO YOUR TABLES

You'll need to update an Excel table over time. You'll update your Excel table with fresh data. In the blank area, data will be inserted. The easiest technique is to place data in the table's first blank row. The table's data will be sorted. If you wish to include data in the table's middle, insert a blank row and fill it in. Both Portland, Ma,ine and Portland, Oregon should get the final 3 days of the month. Below are the steps.

Drop-down menu: Portland, Maine worksheet.

Choose A34 (a left-most cell underneath your last row within the table).

Details below:

Maine data Portland

Day	High (°F)	Low (°F)	Rain (inches)	Snow (inches)
29	31.4	13.3	0.12	0.59
30	31.6	3.4	0.08	0.47
31	31.7	13.5	0.12	0.63

Banded rows formatting continues when extra columns are added.

- Drop-down menu: worksheet or Portland.

- Choose A34 (a left-most cell underneath your last row within the table). Details below:

Table Portland, Oregon detail

Day	High (°F)	Low (°F)	Rain (inches)	Snow (inches)
29	48.8	36.2	0.16	0
30	49.0	36.2	0.11	0.32
31	49.1	36.1	0.16	0

4.4 FINDING & EDITING DATA

You'll need to rectify table data mistakes. Visually scanning a table for mistakes is time-consuming and tiring. Excel's Find command helps. Start at the top of your table and go down to ensure all data is covered.

You know that 3.40 degrees were recorded wrongly in Portland, Maine. It was 13.40. Follow these procedures to fix this.

Portland, Maine.

- Press CTRL+HOME to reach the top of your sheet.

- Home ➔ Find & Edit Group ➔ Find.

- 3.40, then Find Next.

Find/Replace
- Click to close the window.

- Day 10's Low column should be 13.4.

- Look for.32 Snow on your Portland, Oregon sheet. Set 0.12 On day 3, check for the error.

Finding & Replacing Data
- Home ➔ Find & Choose ➔ Find.

- Then click Find Next.

- Click Search Next to continue.

- Change files after closing the window.

4.5 FREEZE ROWS & COLUMNS

When users freeze windows, columns and rows in their table stay visible while they click. If the spreadsheet's initial row has column labels, they should freeze each row to keep them visible as they scroll. That'd be good if you could keep column heads apparent when scrolling over weather data.

To freeze headings:
- Click A6's leftmost cell underneath the heading lines.

- Select View from the ribbon.

- Freeze Panes twice.

- When you scroll your sheet, headers remain at the end.

Click the View tab to unfreeze headers.
Unfreeze panes.

4.6 SIMPLE SORT

Tables may be sorted alphabetically, numerically, or in other ways. Sorting orders table data by one or more columns. The table below gives sort orders for each column.

Table Sort Options

Sort Order	Text	Numbers	Dates
Ascending	Alphabetical (A to Z)	Smallest-Largest	Chronological (oldest-newest)
		Lowest-Highest	
Descending	Reverse Alphabetical (Z to A)	Largest-Smallest	Reverse Chronological (newest-oldest)
		Highest-Lowest	

If you want to discover which day in January in Portland, Maine, received the most snow, sort the Snow column in descending order.
Click the filter. In Portland M E, click Snow's down arrow (inches).
Click a choice. Pick ZA. Largest-smallest. The figure shows more.

EXCEL 2022

If you make an error, you'll notice that January 3rd (row 6) had 0.73" of snow. In the snow section, a filter arrow changes to a downward arrow, signifying declining order (largest-smallest).

Day	High (°F)	Low (°F)	Rain (inches)	Snow (inches)
		National Weather Data		
		January Daily Normals		
		Portland, Maine		
3	32.1	14.6	0.11	0.73
5	31.8	14.2	0.12	0.71
12	30.9	13.2	0.12	0.71
16	30.7	12.9	0.12	0.71
18	30.6	12.8	0.12	0.71
22	30.8	12.8	0.08	0.71
10	31.1	13.4	0.12	0.67

To find Oregon's snowiest day, sort a Portland sheet. Check your answers using the chart below.

Day	High (°F)	Low (°F)	Rain (inches)	Snow (inches)
		National Weather Data		
		January Daily Normals		
		Portland, Oregon		
30	49.0	36.2	0.11	0.32
3	45.2	35.0	0.16	0.12
15	46.8	35.9	0.16	0.11
9	46.0	35.5	0.16	0.08
25	48.3	36.2	0.12	0.08
1	45.0	34.9	0.16	0.00
2	45.1	35.0	0.19	0.00

Sorting the Column

Click the filter. To sort, click the header arrow.

Choose AZ or ZA from the drop-down menu to sort that column.

4.7 MULTI-LEVEL SORT

You may need to filter the table by many columns for optimal data interpretation. If you were looking at several loan categories from multiple bank offices, you'd need to filter by loan form and bank officer's name. If you have a list student'sts' high school grades, you want to sort them by student name and grade level (first-year student, sophomore, junior, senior) so grades are consecutive.

Let's look at Oregon's snow days and see how chilly they were.

Press a table cell on your sheet or Portland.

In the ribbon, click Data and Sort.
Column: Snow.
Order by Largest-Smallest.
Click Add Levels in a dialogue box to add a second level type.
Click Low (°F) for a Column in new, now by lines.
Order a comparable row by Smallest-Largest. Below is a dialogue box.

Okay. Your table type should look like the one below. From Day9's low of 35.50 to Day25's low of 36.20, 0.08" of snow falls. The lowest score was first. The selection arrows on sorted columns have been changed to show how effectively they're sorted.

Day	High (°F)	Low (°F)	Rain (inches)	Snow (inches)
		National Weather Data		
		January Daily Normals		
		Portland, Oregon		
30	49.0	36.2	0.11	0.32
3	45.2	35.0	0.16	0.12
15	46.8	35.9	0.18	0.11
9	46.0	35.5	0.16	0.08
25	48.3	36.2	0.12	0.08
1	48.0	34.9	0.16	0.00
2	45.1	35.0	0.19	0.00
4	45.3	35.1	0.16	0.00
5	45.4	35.2	0.20	0.00

4.8 CUSTOM SORTS

In certain cases, you choose "conventional" data order: highest-lowest quantities, alphabetical words, etc. Sorting daily data this way makes little sense. Friday, Monday, Thursday, Tuesday, Saturday, Sunday, and Wednesday are alphabetically sorted. This request isn't profitable. Alphabetizing a year's months is also confusing. Is there a high-low or low-high sum that seems reasonable? (Great puzzle!)

You've added a weekday column to your weather information and updated it Sunday through Saturday. This sheet enables everyone to examine Portland, Oregon's weekly weather trends. Let's organize the sheet by Week or Day.

- Drop-down menu: Weekly worksheet.

- Insert A5 table.

- Sort on the ribbon's Data tab.

- Column: Week.

- Order by Smallest-Largest.

- To add a second level sort, click Add Level in a dialogue box's top-right corner.

- Choose Day from Column inside new, So by lines.

- Choose Custom List from Order. Below will appear on the screen.

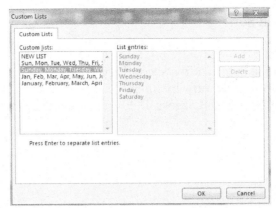

Choose Sunday, Monday, Tuesday, etc., in a dialogue box's Custom list. Choose written days of the week, not acronyms.

After clicking OK, the Sort box should look like this:

OK again. Below is a sorted table. Week-by-week data is grouped by day.

Save it.

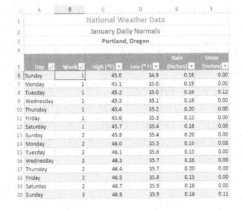

4.9 HOW TO BUILD PIVOT TABLES (BASIC COMMANDS)

Excel's pivot tables are strong. A pivot table helps you analyze huge, comprehensive data sets. 213 records & 6 fields make up our dataset. Amount, Date, ID, Category, and Country.

	A	B	C	D	E	F	G	H
1	Order ID	Product	Category	Amount	Date	Country		
2	1	Carrots	Vegetables	$4,270	1/6/2016	United States		
3	2	Broccoli	Vegetables	$8,239	1/7/2016	United Kingdom		
4	3	Banana	Fruit	$617	1/8/2016	United States		
5	4	Banana	Fruit	$8,384	1/10/2016	Canada		
6	5	Beans	Vegetables	$2,626	1/10/2016	Germany		
7	6	Orange	Fruit	$3,610	1/11/2016	United States		
8	7	Broccoli	Vegetables	$9,062	1/11/2016	Australia		
9	8	Banana	Fruit	$6,906	1/16/2016	New Zealand		
10	9	Apple	Fruit	$2,417	1/16/2016	France		
11	10	Apple	Fruit	$7,431	1/16/2016	Canada		

Insert your Pivot Table

Steps for inserting a pivot table.

1. Select a data set cell.

2. Click PivotTable under Insert > Tables.

- This box appears. Excel auto-selects data. The new pivot table defaults to New Worksheet.

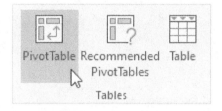

- Clink on, OK

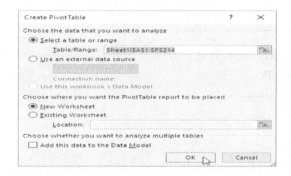

Drag fields

PivotTable Fields opens. Drag the following fields to determine every product's export total.

1. Add Product to Rows.

2. Add the amount to values.

3. Country to Filters.

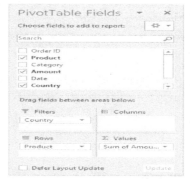

The table pivot is below. You export mostly bananas. Pivot tables are that simple.

	A	B	C
1	Country	(All)	
2			
3	Row Labels	Sum of Amount	
4	Apple	191257	
5	Banana	340295	
6	Beans	57281	
7	Broccoli	142439	
8	Carrots	136945	
9	Mango	57079	
10	Orange	104438	
11	**Grand Total**	**1029734**	
12			

Sort

Sort your pivot table to put Banana first.

1. Click a Sum of Amount cell.

2. Click Sort, Largest to Smallest.

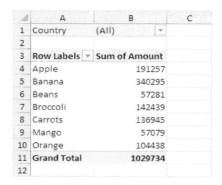

Result.

	A	B	C
1	Country	(All)	
2			
3	Row Labels	Sum of Amount	
4	Banana	340295	
5	Apple	191257	
6	Broccoli	142439	
7	Carrots	136945	
8	Orange	104438	
9	Beans	57281	
10	Mango	57079	
11	**Grand Total**	**1029734**	
12			

Filter

You can filter your pivot table per Country since you added it to Filters. What do we export to France most?

1. Click your France filter.

Result. France's top import is apples.

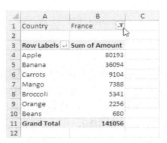

Change Summary Calculations

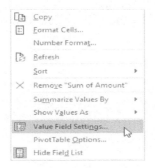

Excel sums or counts data by default. Follow these procedures to update your calculations.

1. Click a Sum of Amount cell.

2. Right-click Value Field Settings.

3. Choose a computation. Click Count.

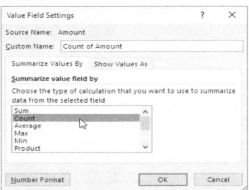

4. Click on OK.

The third step is to decide on the kind of computation to be used. Count, for instance, is an example.

Two-dimensional Pivot Tables

With the Columns & Rows areas, you may build the two-dimensional pivot tables by dragging a field. Make use of the convenience of a pivot table by doing so first. To find out how much of each commodity was shipped to each nation, move the following fields around.

1. The Rows location is surrounded by farmland.

2. An additional column for products.

3. To the Values box, add the Amount field.

4. The category field has been added to the Filters section.

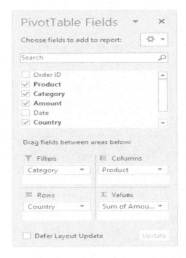

A two-dimensional pivot table is shown below.

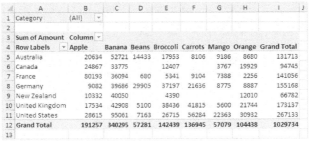

	A	B	C	D	E	F	G	H	I	J
1	Category	(All)								
2										
3	Sum of Amount	Column								
4	Row Labels	Apple	Banana	Beans	Broccoli	Carrots	Mango	Orange	Grand Total	
5	Australia	20634	52721	14433	17953	8106	9186	8680	131713	
6	Canada	24867	33775		12407		3767	19929	94745	
7	France	80193	36094	680	5341	9104	7388	2256	141056	
8	Germany	9082	39686	29905	37197	21636	8775	8887	155168	
9	New Zealand	10332	40050		4390			12010	66782	
10	United Kingdom	17534	42908	5100	38436	41815	5600	21744	173137	
11	United States	28615	95061	7163	26715	56284	22363	30932	267133	
12	Grand Total	191257	340295	57281	142439	136945	57079	104438	1029734	
13										

The best way to compare these figures is to build your pivot chart & add a filter. This may be a phase too much for you at this point, but it demonstrates to you one of the numerous strong pivot table capabilities that Excel has to offer.

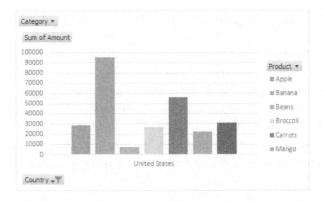

CHAPTER 5: CHARTS & GRAPHS

Charts & graphs help you comprehend outcomes by visualizing numbers. These terms are different despite being regularly interchanged. Graphs are the easiest way to visually depict numbers over time. Charts are more sophisticated since they help compare data sets. Charts are more attractive than diagrams since they don't employ x- and y-axes.

In reports, charts & graphs are used to show management, customers, or team members' progress or results. You can construct a chart or graph to illustrate any statistical data, saving you time searching through spreadsheets to uncover links and trends.

Excel makes it simple to create charts & graphs, especially when you keep the data in your Excel Workbook. Excel provides various pre-made chart & graph types from which to pick.

5.1 TIRED OF THOSE STATIC SPREADSHEETS?

Microsoft Excel wasn't designed to manage tasks. Examine Excel vs. Smartsheet's work management, accessibility, collaboration, visibility, and integrations.

5.2 IN EXCEL WHEN TO MAKE CHART & GRAPH TYPE

Excel's chart and graph library let you graphically present findings. It's important to choose a chart style that tells the narrative you want your data to tell. Vector graphics should be used to improve charts and graphs. Microsoft Excel 2016 has 5 chart types:

Column Charts: Column charts are extensively used to analyze data or divide one component into numerous parts (for instance, multiple genres or products). Excel's 7-column chart formats are clustered, staggered, 100% stacked, 3D stacked, 3D clustered, and 3D 100% stacked. Choose the best visualization for your findings.

Bar Chart: Bars in a bar chart are horizontal, whereas columns are vertical. Bar charts and column charts may be used equally, while some

prefer column charts for visualizing negative numbers on a y-axis.

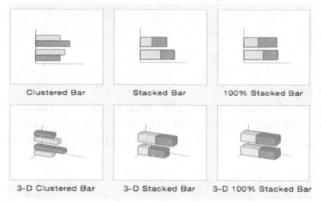

Pie Charts: Pie charts measure the proportion of the entire (many data values). A pie crust represents each concept, showing proportions. There are approximately five pie charts: pie, pie (which splits a pie in half to show subcategory proportions), a bar of the pie, 3D pies, and doughnut.

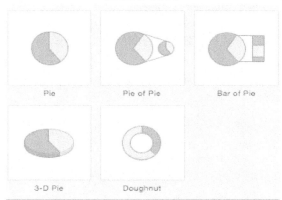

Line Charts: Line charts show temporal patterns instead of static data points. The lines connect every data point, showing whether values improved or fell over time. 7-line chart versions include line, 100% stacked line, stacked line, line with markers, stacked line with markers, & 3D line.

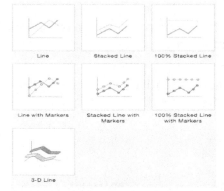

Scatter Charts: Scattered charts show the relationship between variables. They assist show development over time like line diagrams. (Correlation) Bubble charts are scattered. Seven scatter chart options include smooth lines & markers, straight lines, bubbles, and 3D bubbles.

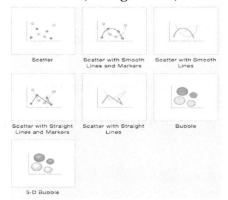

In addition, there are 4 minor divisions. These graphs are more case-specific:

Area charts: These charts, like line charts, show value fluctuations over time. Since the area beneath each line is solid, area charts illustrate transitions across numerous variables. 6 areas include area, 100% stacked area, 3D area, and 3D 100% stacked area.

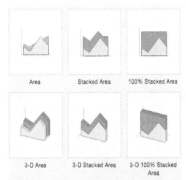

Stock: This graphic shows a stock's high, low, and closing prices in financial reports and by investors. You may utilize a value range (or predicted value range) and its precise value in every circumstance.

Open-high-low-close, volume-high-low-close, high-low-close, & volume-open-high-low-close are chart options.

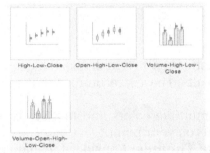

Surface: This surface chart displays data in 3D. Wide data sets with more than 2 variables and data sets with groups benefit from the extra plane. Surface charts may be hard to comprehend, so ensure your audience is comfortable. Wireframe 3D surface, contour, and wireframe contour are all available.

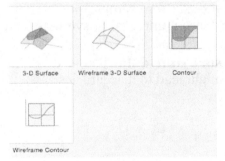

Radar: A radar map compares many variables. All variables start at the center. The key to utilizing a radar chart is comparing all elements; they're often used to compare items or personnel. Charts might be radar, radar with marks, or filled radar.

The waterfall chart displays positive and negative gains over time using column graphs. You may download a tutorial to help easily create a waterfall map in Excel.

5.3 TOP FIVE EXCEL CHART & GRAPH BEST TRAINING

Excel has many styles, and stylistic presets to enhance table appearance and readability but utilizing them doesn't ensure the best results. These 5 recommended practices will make your chart & graph as easy and useful as feasible.

Clean It Up: Diagrams with multiple colors and text are confusing and don't stick out. Remove distractions so viewers may focus on your point.

Select the Most Appropriate Themes: Consider the audience, topic, or chart's main goal when picking a theme. Try out several models but choose one that fits your requirements.

Use Text Carefully: Maps and graphs are visual, although the text may be included (like axis labels or titles). Be succinct, clear, and thoughtful about each document's orientation (it's not comfortable to switch heads to read text on the x-axis, for example).

Place Elements Carefully: Place names, tales, symbols, and other graphics carefully. They may enhance the graph.

Before making the chart, sort your data: People don't filter their data or eliminate duplicates until they make a map, which might lead to inaccuracies.

5.4 HOW YOU CAN CHART DATA WITHIN EXCEL

You must first provide Excel with some data to work with before you can construct an Excel chart or graph. With this chapter, you'll discover how to chart data in Excel 2016.

Step1: Enter Data in a Worksheet

- Excel File ➜ New Workbook.

- Input data for a graph or map. In this situation, you're comparing 2013-2017 goods. Number all columns and rows. You may then create charts and graphs using basic axis markings.

	A	B	C	D	E	F
1	Product ▼	2013 ▼	2014 ▼	2015 ▼	2016 ▼	2017 ▼
2	Product A	$18,580	$49,225	$16,326	$10,017	$26,134
3	Product B	$78,970	$82,262	$48,640	$48,640	$48,640
4	Product C	$24,236	$131,390	$79,022	$71,009	$81,474
5	Product D	$16,730	$19,730	$12,109	$11,355	$17,686
6	Product E	$35,358	$42,685	$20,893	$16,065	$21,388
7						

Step2: Select any Range to make a Chart and Graph from the Workbook Data

- By highlighting the data cells, you want to include in the graph.

- After highlighting a cell, pick a chart form.

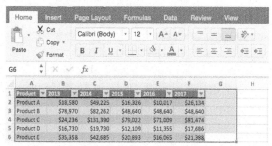

This chapter covers building a chart (clustered column) in Excel.

5.5 HOW YOU CAN MAKE YOUR CHART THROUGH EXCEL

After entering data and selecting a cell set, choose a chart form. The following example creates a chart (clustered column) using prior data.

Step1: Select the Chart Type

Click Insert until your data is outlined in Workbook. The toolbar's middle has various chart options. You may pick a different Recommended Chart by using the drop-down choices.

Step2: Create Your desired Chart

Insert → Column Chart → Clustered Column.

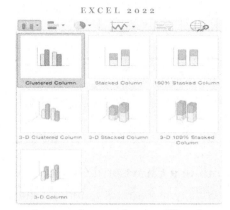

Using your data, Excel can create a cluster chart column. The chart will be in the center. Double-click a Chart Title and input a tag. "Product Profit 2013-2017" describes this graph.

This chart will guide a walkthrough. Download the chart to continue.

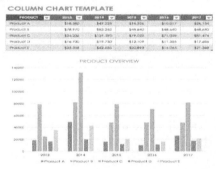

Cart Design & Format are toolbar components for making chart adjustments. By default, Excel applies a predefined style, layout, and format to charts & graphs; you may alter them using tabs. Then you'll see Chart Design choices.

Step3: Add the Chart Elements

Adding chart components to a graph or chart may clarify or add significance. Choose a chart element from the top-left Add Chart Feature drop-down menu (below your home tab).

To Hide or Display Axes:

Choose axes. Excel will automatically grab column and row headers from your selected cell set to display horizontal and vertical axes (check Primary Horizontal & Primary Vertical under Axes).

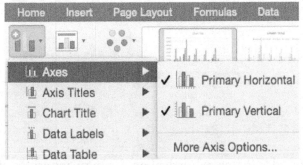

Uncheck these to remove the chart's view axis. Selecting Primary Horizontal removes the years from the horizontal axis.

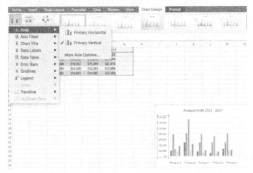

More Axis Choices... displays a window with more formatting & text choices, such as identifiers, numbers, tick marks, or altering text color & height.

To Add the Axis Titles:

After selecting Add Chart Element, choose Axis Title. Since Excel doesn't automatically assign axis names, Primary Horizontal or Primary Vertical are unregulated.

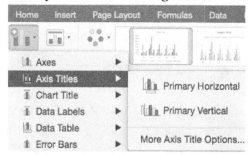

Pressing Primary Horizontal & Primary Vertical on the map generates axis names. Both were pushed. Title axis. You added "Year" and "Profit."

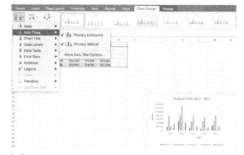

To Move or Remove Chart Title:

Add Chart Elements drop-down menu: Chart Title. None, Above the Chart, Focused Overlay, & Further Title Choices.

Selecting None deletes the chart title.

Click the Above Chart to add a title. Excel may automatically add a chart's title above it.

Choose Centered Overlay to center the chart's title. Be careful not to obscure data or clutter the graph with your title (like in this example below).

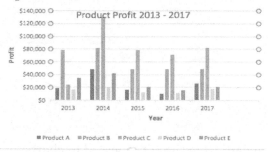

To Add the Data Labels:

Add Chart Elements ➔ Data Labels. There are 6 data labels: Inside End, Outside End, Inside Base, & More Label titles.

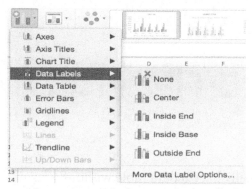

The 4 placement options give each computed data point a distinctive mark. Choose one. This adjustment may be handy if you have few details or plenty of chart space. The graphic (clumped column) would seem overloaded with data labels. So does picking the Center data label.

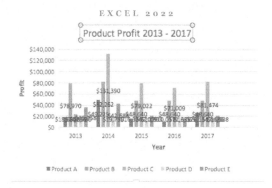

To Add the Data Table:

Add Chart Elements ➔ Data Table. Further Data Table Choices offers 3 pre-formatted alternatives and an enlarged menu.

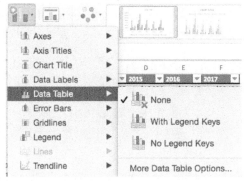

None is the default value, so data tables aren't repeated in charts.

Legend Keys displays a data table underneath the list. The legend is color-coded.

No Legend Keys charts typically have a data table without a legend.

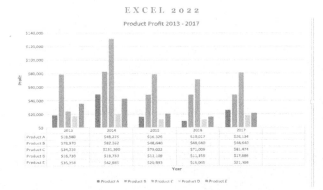

If you need to add a data table, enlarge your chart. Click a corner to scale your chart.

To Add the Error Bars:

Add Chart Elements ➔ Error Bars. None (default), 5% (Percentage), Standard Error, & Standard Deviation. Inaccuracy bars show the probable error in reported results using conventional formulae.

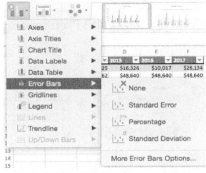

When you choose Standard Errors, a chart appears.

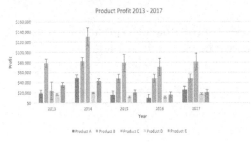

To Add the Gridlines:

Add Chart Elements & Gridlines adds gridlines to a chart. Prime Major Horizontal, Prime Major Vertical, Prime Minor Horizontal, & Prime Minor Vertical. Excel adds a horizontal gridline to column tables.

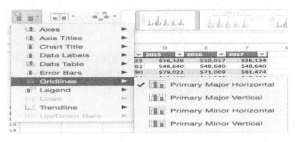

You may choose as many gridlines as you wish using the options. Here's your chart with all 4 gridlines chosen.

To Add the Legend:

Add Chart Elements ➜ Legend. Contrary to Legend Preferences, there are 5 legend placement options: None, Correct, Top, Left, and Bottom.

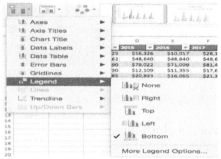

The legend's placement depends on the chart's type and format. Choose the best graph option. This is how your chart appears when you press the Right legend.

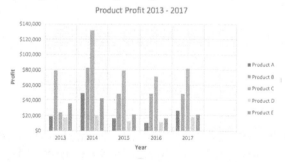

Clustered column charts don't support lines (clustered). In certain chart categories, you should add lines by selecting the correct answer (e.g., goal, average, comparison, etc.).

To Add the Trendline:

Add Chart Elements ➜ Trendline. There are 5 options: None (default), Linear Forecast, Linear, Exponential, and Moving Average. Use the correct data-collection instrument. Choose Linear.

Excel gives trendlines for 5 distinct items when compared over time. Click a product's blue OK button to construct linear trendlines.

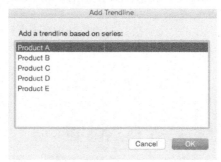

Now your chart will show Product A's linear growth with dotted trendlines. Excel's legend has Linear (A Product) applied.

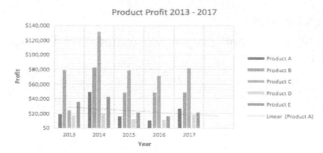

Double-click trendlines to reveal trendline equations. Format Trendlines may appear on the right. Check the box below. Display equation on chart. The chart now shows the equation.

Each chart characteristic may have as many trendlines as desired. Here's a graphic showing A&C's trendlines.

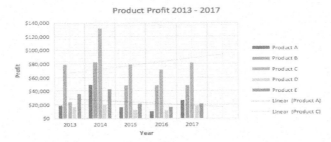

Up/Down Bars can't be used in column charts, but they may be used in line charts to show data point climbs and drops.

Step4: Adjust a Quick Layout

Quick Layout is the toolbar's second drop-down option that lets you arrange chart components (legend, titles, clusters, etc.).

Eleven layouts are available. Hover over each option for a description, then choose it.

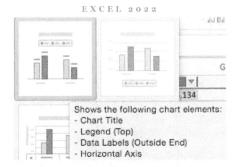

Step5: Change the Colors

In the toolbar, choose Colors. Choose the finest color scheme (these may be aesthetic and complement the colors & theme of your brand).

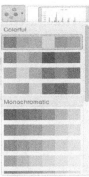

Step6: Change the Style

Charts employ 14 forms (cluster column). The chart defaults to Style 1, but you may change it. Click the photo bar's right arrow for more options.

Step7: Switch Column/Row

To rotate the axis, click Switch Row/Column. If you have more than 2 variables, switching axes isn't intuitive.

Switch
Row/Column

Switching column and row reverses the product and year (profit remains on your y-axis). The graph is now arranged by product (not by year), and the legend is color-coded (not-product). To avoid confusion, change Series to Years in legend.

Step8: Select the Data

Click Select Data on your toolbar to change the file context.

Wide-swinging doors. When you're done, click Ok. The table would automatically reflect the newest data.

Step9: Change the Chart Type

Change the chart type.

Here you may change Excel's 9 chart kinds. Check that the data fits your chart format.

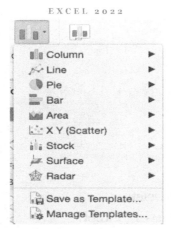

Save the chart as a template by clicking Save as...

You'll be prompted to name your design. Excel can construct model folders for rapid organization. To save, click Save.

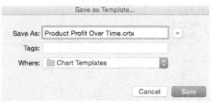

Step10: Move the Chart

Click Move Chart in the rightmost toolbar.

You may place the chart in a conversation box. You may use this map to create a new layer or as an object in another sheet. Press blue OK to continue.

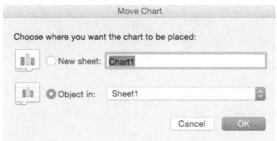

Step11: Change the Formatting

The Format tab lets you change the colors, size, design, fill, and orientation of chart components and text and insert objects. To construct a brand map, click Format and use a shortcut (images, colors, etc.).

Choose the chart feature to update from the toolbar's drop-down menu.

Step12: Delete the Chart

To remove a chart, select it and hit Delete.

How can you make the Graph using Excel?

Excel groups graph into chart categories because graphs and charts are distinct. Follow these instructions to create a graph or chart.

To make a graph with workbook data, select a range

Highlight cells with the data, you want on the graph.
Illuminate the grayed-out cell spectrum.

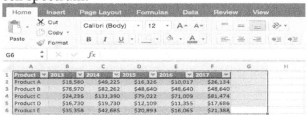

After outlining, pick a graph (Excel refers to a chart). Insert tab, Recommended Charts. Choose a graph type.

The graph appears onscreen. Repeat the preceding steps to customize your graph. All graph-making routines are the same.

CHAPTER 6: DATA MANAGEMENT TECHNIQUES

In this chapter, you will learn about multiple data management techniques including data validation and rules to validate your data, data formatting,g and consolidation, and, data analysis.

6.1 DATA VALIDATION & RULES

Excel's Data Validation tool helps users input reliable data. Data validation limits what may be input in a cell and provides guidelines.

Create a Validation Rule

- Decide which cells you'd want to verify.

- Go to the Data tab by clicking on it.

- Click on the button Data Validation.

- A selection of options will appear.

- Choice the form of data that you command to let in.

Any value: Not validation criteria were applied.

Whole number: Allows any number between 0 and the specified minimum/maximum.
Decimals and percentages may be input as decimals within the defined limitations.

List: Select a value from the drop-down menu. Users may choose from a list by clicking on the list arrow in the cell.

Date: Permits a specific date if it's not outside the specified range.

Time: Permits a certain amount of time if it's not exceeded.

Text length: Permits a specified number of characters to be entered.

Custom: A formula might be entered to compute what is permitted in the cell.

Give specifics on how the data will be validated.

Depending on the Allow option chosen, the validation choices will be different.

Then press the OK button.

Set cell data validation (s). Excel prevents invalid data entering and displays a notification about the restricted cell.

To discover verified data inside a worksheet, select Find & Choose and choose Data Validation. Highlighted verified cells.

Add Input & Error Messages

Set Excel to show a notification when a cell or range is chosen to prevent data validation errors. These notifications help when others input data into your spreadsheet. Invalid data might trigger an error message.

- Select the cells in which you wish to see an input message.

- Go to the Data tab by clicking on it.

- Click on the Data Validation button.

- Input Message is on the left-hand side.

- Input a message here.

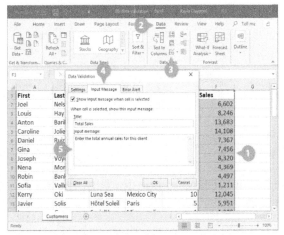

Look at the Error Alert section.

Select the kind of error message that should be shown to the user.

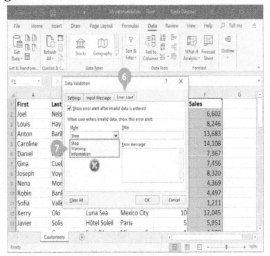

Stop: Prevents the entry of incorrect data into a cell by a user.

Warning: The user can accept an invalid input, change it, or cancel the process.

Information: Users are given the option of either clicking OK to approve the incorrect input or clicking Cancel to get it removed.

- Enter a warning message in the field.

- Then press the OK button.

- Select any cell containing a text you need to enter.

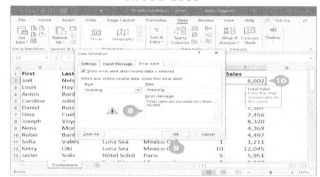

Selecting a cell within range now creates a pop-up with the range's title and message. The custom warning message is shown if an incorrect value is entered.

Rules

You must develop data-validation criteria in Excel since inputting data is so boring. Data validation rules are essential. A data-validation rule specifies what may be entered in a cell.

Here's what to type when you choose a cell with a rule. An error message appears if you input data improperly.

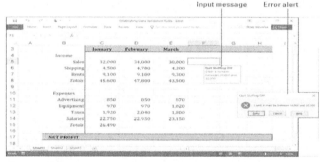

A data-validation rule in action.

Data validation procedures prevent careless data input and that uncomfortable sensation during tedious tasks. In a date cell, you may need dates.

In a text-entry cell, you may pick an element from a list. In numeric cells, you may set a range. The table lists data-validation categories.

Data-Validation Rule Categories	
Rule	**What Can Be Entered**
Any Value	Anything whatsoever. This is the default setting.
Whole Number	Whole numbers (no decimal points allowed). Choose an operator from the Data drop-down list and values to describe the range of numbers that can be entered.
Decimal	Same as the Whole Number rule except numbers with decimal points are permitted.
List	Items from a list. Enter the list items in cells on a worksheet, either the one you're working in or another. Then reopen the Data Validation dialog box, click the Range Selector button (you can find it on the right side of the Source text box), and select the cells that hold the list. The list items appear in a drop-down list on the worksheet.
Date	Date values. Choose an operator from the Data drop-down list and values to describe the date range. Earlier in this chapter, "Entering date and time values" describes the correct way to enter date values.
Time	Time values. Choose an operator from the Data drop-down list and values to describe the date and time range. Earlier in this chapter, "Entering date and time values" describes the correct way to enter a combination of date and time values.
Text Length	A certain number of characters. Choose an operator from the Data drop-down list and values to describe how many characters can be entered.
Custom	A logical value (True or False). Enter a formula that describes what constitutes a true or false data entry.

Set a data-validation rule using these steps.

- Choose the needed cells.

- Click Data Validation under Data.

- Data Validation dialogue box Settings tab.

The Data Validation dialogue box's Settings tab.

- Use the Allow drop-down menu to choose the rule type you wish to apply.

- Specify the rule's parameters here.

- For each rule category, the criterion is different. The table explains how to input the criteria for each rule type. The worksheet's cells may be referenced by clicking on them. To do so, you may either choose them straight or select the Ranges Selector button & select them.

- Enter a title and a message in the Input Message field.

- For example, "Quit Slacking Off" is prominently displayed on the page. The title has been bolded out. Tell us more about the kind of data you chose for the cell(s).

- A warning message may be added to the Message Alert dialogue box by using the Error Alert tab's style, title, and message fields.

- The stop was selected within the error message given before. The message shows next to the symbol, and the title that enters appears across the top of the dialogue box to the left.

- Right-click to accept.

- Remove data-validation rules by selecting the cells, going to the Data tab, and clicking Data Validation, then on the Settings tab of the Data Validation dialogue box, clicking Clear All, and then clicking OK.

6.2 DATA FORMATTING & CONSOLIDATION

You may use Data Consolidation to combine data from many worksheets into a single expert worksheet. If you have a lot of different spreadsheets or workbooks, you may use the Data Consolidation feature to combine all the information into a single spreadsheet.

Data Consolidation may be challenging to deal with, but don't give up. Data Consolidation is a powerful tool that may help you rapidly and effectively analyze and display your data. Good groundwork is the key to accomplishment, no matter how frightening the screen may seem at first.

Using this example, you'll learn from one of your Excel experts how to organize the data before summarizing it to make your findings more comprehensible.

The following is what you'll be looking at:

- Workbook consolidation by merging data from numerous worksheets.

- In a new worksheet, merging the data from numerous spreadsheets into a single summary

Versions 2007 and later Excel versions are all compatible with the steps below. This advice might not function if you use Excel 2003 or an earlier program version.

Multiple worksheets in the same workbook may have their data combined using

In this example, you can see how much you spent on tea, coffee, & milk over the last three years. One year's worth of data is divided into quarters and kept on a single worksheet every quarter in one workbook.

It is possible to construct an annual or quarterly "Consolidated Summary" that shows all your expenses in one place. It doesn't matter whether the columns and rows are arranged similarly. Excel can take care of it. Amazing!

Year 1 worksheet

	A	B	C	D	E
1		Quarter 1	Quarter 2	Quarter 3	Quarter 4
2	Coffee	£ 2,128	£ 3,526	£ 5,372	£ 9,378
3	Tea	£ 1,633		£ 5,392	£ 1,730
4	Milk	£ 4,837		£ 3,082	£ 5,272

Year 1 | Year 2 | Year 3 | Consolidated Summary | (+)

Year 2 worksheet

	A	B	C	D	E
8		Quarter 1	Quarter 2	Quarter 3	Quarter 4
9	Coffee	£ 2,944	£ 3,528	£ 7,822	£ 8,464
10	Milk	£ 8,227		£ 9,462	£ 2,748
11					

Year 1 | Year 2 | Year 3 | Consolidated Summary | (+)

Year 3 worksheet

	Quarter 4	Quarter 3	Quarter 1
8 Coffee	£ 9,664	£ 7,123	£ 2,643
9 Tea	£ 7,356	£ 2,865	£ 6,092
10 Milk	£ 6,787	£ 1,595	£ 8,356
11			

Year 1 | Year 2 | Year 3 | Consolidated Summary

Columns & rows are arranged differently in Years 1, 2, & 3, as seen in the table. For example, in Year two, there is no tea, and in Year Three, there isn't any Quarter Two & the Quarters aren't in sequence. Consolidated ranges need not be the same dimension in each worksheet; the number of columns or rows may vary from one worksheet to the next. You may create a summary sheet by condensing all the data. What a fantastic discovery!

Consolidation step:

Use an active worksheet or generate a new one if required as your master worksheet before using the Data Consolidation tool. A new title for the worksheet is 'Consolidated Summary.

Ensure the upper-left cell in the region where the aggregated data will be shown is selected.

To see the Consolidate dialogue, choose Data ➔ Consolidate on the Ribbon.

Excel will aggregate the data using the summary function you provide in the Function box. Eleven functions are available, as you can see in the drop-down menu. You'll use the Sum function since you'll add the numbers in your dataset.

You may add the first piece of data to a consolidation dialogue by selecting it within the Reference area & then dragging the data (containing column and row headers) over to the Sheet tab and clicking the Add button.

You may keep doing this until you have all your information listed under "References," such as "Year 2" & "Year 3," by selecting the following page and then selecting the data on it with your mouse.

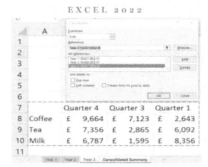

		Quarter 4		Quarter 3		Quarter 1
8	Coffee	£	9,664	£ 7,123	£	2,643
9	Tea	£	7,356	£ 2,865	£	6,092
10	Milk	£	6,787	£ 1,595	£	8,356

To get the most out of the Consolidation process, you may name the ranges before you begin the procedure. Consolidation may be done by pressing F3 within the Reference field and selecting the range from the Paste Name dialogue box if you have named each range.

Select the checkboxes under Use tags in the top row, left column, & to show where the labels are contained in the source ranges. Quarter1, Quarter2, etc., are shown in the top row, whereas the products listed in the left column are, for example, coffee, tea, and milk.

What's the difference between automatic and manual updates? Select the Create connections to original data tick box if you want Excel to update the consolidation table automatically as the source data changes. If this option is unchecked, you may still manually update your consolidation.

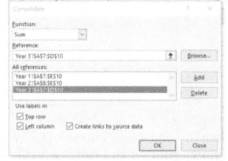

Excel creates a new page for you to use as the master worksheet when you click OK (Consolidated Summary).

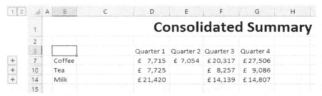

Consolidated Summary

		Quarter 1	Quarter 2	Quarter 3	Quarter 4
7	Coffee	£ 7,715	£ 7,054	£ 20,317	£ 27,506
10	Tea	£ 7,725		£ 8,257	£ 9,086
14	Milk	£ 21,420		£ 14,139	£ 14,807

You'll see something new in the Excel spreadsheet that you haven't seen before. To show and conceal data, utilize the grouping tools on the left side of the screen. Rows 7, 10, and 14 all have plus signs next to them. In this case, the cells are components of a collapsing group. When you click the + symbol, you'll see a line that connects all rows to the left:

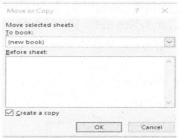

Column C of data indicates the workbook name (Column C) that includes the data. If you don't want to see this column, just right-click on it and choose Hide. This merely conceals the column so you can still access the data if needed.

Copying the worksheets to a new workbook

Once again, having everything planned out ahead of time will be beneficial.

As you'll see, several entries in your Consolidated Summary aren't useful. Because range C4: C6 displays just the workbook's title, it's difficult to tell where the numbers in the range D4: G6 originate. You should consider separating all worksheets into independent workbooks before applying data consolidation if the source data is included on the summary page. To help you out, here are some instructions.

You will copy your selected worksheet into some new workbook; now, select from your book drop-down categories. Select a Create the copy box. Because you're creating a new workbook, there are no worksheets within Before sheet lists before which you can insert a copied worksheet. This will be the only worksheet within the new workbook.

Click Yes. The worksheet gets copied into a new workbook created for this purpose. The worksheet will be removed from the original workbook if you want to relocate it. Save the current workbook as "Year 1.xls" after copying a worksheet. Workbooks for years two and three should be called Year 2.xls (for the second year) & Year 3.xls (for the third year), accordingly. As laborious as this may be at first, it will pay off in the long run!

Join numerous workbooks together into a single new one.

To aggregate several open workbooks, make sure they are all open.

Keep your master worksheet in an empty spreadsheet or create a new one if needed. Worksheet "Consolidate Summary" has been changed to "Consolidate Summary" and saved as Summary.xls in the new workbook.

Ensure the upper-left cell in the region where the aggregated data will be shown is selected.

Data > Consolidate on the Ribbon and may be accessed by clicking the Consolidate button.

The only difference is that you pick data ranges from separate workbooks instead of distinct worksheets, as you did in the previous example.

When you select OK, Excel creates a new master worksheet with all the data you entered (Consolidated Summary).

Consolidated Summary

		Quarter 1	Quarter 2	Quarter 3	Quarter 4
	Year 1	£ 2,128	£ 3,526	£ 5,372	£ 9,378
	Year 2	£ 2,944	£ 3,528	£ 7,822	£ 8,464
	Year 3	£ 2,643		£ 7,123	£ 9,664
Coffee		£ 7,715	£ 7,054	£20,317	£27,506
	Year 1	£ 1,633		£ 5,392	£ 1,730
	Year 3	£ 6,092		£ 2,865	£ 7,356
Tea		£ 7,725		£ 8,257	£ 9,086
	Year 1	£ 4,837		£ 3,082	£ 5,272
	Year 2	£ 8,227		£ 9,462	£ 2,748
	Year 3	£ 8,356		£ 1,595	£ 6,787
Milk		£21,420		£14,139	£14,807

Column C now displays the name of a workbook that contains your data, which is more useful than the previous example.

6.3 HOW TO ANALYZE DATA IN EXCEL

In every field, people utilize Microsoft Excel as a standard piece of software. Some excel with crucial tables and histograms, while others stick to pie charts & conditional formatting as their primary tools.

Excel may be used for data analysis, but it can also be used as a canvas for artistic expression. Microsoft Excel and its usefulness will be examined in depth in this session. This lesson will go through the many tips and tactics for analyzing Excel analytics data. Excel data analysis techniques will also be discussed.

We'll go through several Excel analytics capabilities to better understand how to analyze data in Excel, functions, and best practices.

Making the Pivot Table a Best Friend

You can quickly and easily summarize massive volumes of data using a pivot tool. One of Excel's most useful tools is identifying and analyzing dataset trends.

It's easy to see trends in a tiny dataset. However, the sheer size of the datasets necessitates more work to uncover any trends. To sum up large amounts of data in just a few minutes utilizing a pivot table is a big benefit. An example of data analysis can be found using a dataset of regions and the number of sales. A breakdown of sales by region might help you figure out what's going wrong in a particular location and what you can do to fix it. You may quickly and easily build an excel report and save it for future use using a pivot table.

Using a Pivot Table, you may average, sum, or count data from another spreadsheet or table in Excel. Using this tool, you can organize and display data rapidly, which is useful for swiftly producing reports.

The spreadsheet you've put up may be copied and pasted into Excel or Google Docs (simply click File ➔ Make one Copy) if you need to use it in another program.

You will find information on a fictitious company's customers in the spreadsheet. For rapid analysis, we may use a pivot table to aggregate this data to view the total transactions per firm and evaluate purchases across various organizations.

Using the Pivot table, you may reorganize a table with several data in it so that you can only see the information that is relevant to you.

If you're using a Mac or PC, you may pick the whole dataset and choose "Data" ➔ "Pivot Table" from the drop-down menu. A table should open in a new tab when you press that.

Data Set

b) When you have the table next to you, you may drag & drop your Row Labels, Column Labels, & Report Filter.

- Your table's top row is occupied with column labels (for example, Company Name, Date, Month)

- For example, dates, months, and your company's name are good candidates for row labels that run the length of your table on the left side.

- Data that you want to be analyzed is entered here (for example, Revenue, Purchases)

- Refine your findings using the Report Filter. About anything goes here

The data in your reports may be easily organized using pivot tables. Alternatively, you may make a copy inside Google App (File ➔ Make a Copy) by copying and pasting the data.

Analyzing Data Set with Excel

Using Excel, you can quickly generate various graphs, including line & column charts, or even add micrographs to your spreadsheet.

Table styles, PivotTables, fast totals, & conditional formatting are all options. When working with enormous datasets in Excel, there are a few easy principles to remember:

- Identify the cells containing the information in which you are interested.

- To quickly analyze your chosen data, click your Quick Analysis icon picture button (or enter CRTL + Q).

- The Quick Analysis Lens icon is available while viewing selected data.

- Select a tab from the Quick Analysis gallery. For example, you may use Charts to display your data on a graph.

- Choose from one of the choices or point to any of them to get a preview.

- It is possible to note that the possibilities available to you aren't always identical. In many cases, this is because the selections in your worksheet vary according to the kind of data you've chosen.

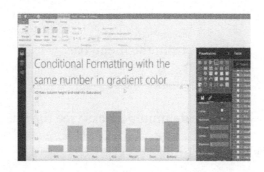

You may want to discover which Excel analysis option is appropriate for you to grasp the best technique to analyze data in Excel. Here, we summarize a few of the most popular solutions.

- **Formatting:** Data bars & colors may be added to your data to make it easier to see what you're looking at. With this, you may instantly view the highest and lowest figures.

- **Charts:** Excel provides various charts depending on the data you've chosen to work with. If you can't find the chart you're looking for, click More Charts to explore more options.

- **Totals:** It is possible to determine the totals for each row and column. Running Total, as an example, inserts a total that increases as new items are added to your data. To show more possibilities, utilize the small black arrows to the right & left of the current selection.

- **Tables:** Filtering and sorting your data is a breeze using tables. More is the option if you don't find the table format you desire.

- **Sparklines:** It is possible to display small graphs, called sparklines, alongside your raw data. Trends may be seen thanks to these tools quickly.

Tips & Tricks

If you know how to play the game, data analysis in MS Excel may be a lot of fun.

Following are some tips on how you can use Excel to evaluate data.

Data Cleaning

One of Excel's most fundamental tasks, data cleaning, is made easier with several helpful tips and tactics. With the help of Power Query, you may master how to do the same thing in Excel. Excel 2016 has a function called Power Query, which is also available as an Add-in for Excel. Your data may be extracted, transformed, and loaded with only a few clicks.

Convert text numbers to numeric formats

When importing data from a non-Excel source, numbers may be imported as text in certain cases. A green popup within the cell's upper-left corner will appear to let you know that an error has occurred.

You may easily convert the values in the range to numbers by selecting 'Convert to a number from the tooltip choices, depending on the number of the range's values.

Excel will take a few extra seconds to complete the conversion if you've over 1000 values.

Using Text-to-Columns and the procedures below, you may convert these values to numeric format:

- You'll need to choose the range of numbers you want to convert.

- Select Data ➜ Text to Columns from the menu bar.

- Once you've selected Delimited, click Next.

- Click Next after clearing all the delimiter checks (see the image below for a visual guide).

- Text-Columns-Checkboxes

Select General & click on the Finish

If you have many numbers to convert, this trick will save you a lot of time. Converting columns in Power Query is as simple as clicking on a column header and right-clicking.

- Then, click on the Change Type option to make the necessary adjustments.

- then choose the type of number you desire (such as a Whole Number or Decimal)

- Power-Query-Datatype

Data Analysis

With Excel analytics, data analysis is simplified and expedited. Here are some pointers for the workplace:

- Excel tables may be used to create auto-expanding ranges. Excel Tables are one of Excel's most underutilized capabilities. Excel's tables include several useful features that make it easier to get things done. The following are only a few of these features:

- Formula It is possible to automatically have a formula duplicated to the remainder of a table after you input it.

- Adding more entries to the table by typing them below or to the right will cause it to expand automatically.

- Your headers will be displayed no matter where you are on the table.

- The sum of a row may be calculated automatically by using the appropriate formula.

- As part of a calculation, you may use Excel tables. Like dropdown lists, formulas that rely on tables will automatically be updated as new entries are added to those tables.

- Create a graphic using data from Excel Tables: Excel Tables may also be used to update charts automatically. There is no requirement to manually update data sources with Excel Tables, as seen in the example.

Data Visualization

Sparklines, a visualization tool of MS Excel, enable you to rapidly view the general trend of a group of information. Mini graphs called sparklines may be found within cells. You may wish to depict the average monthly revenue a team of salespeople generates.

Follow these procedures to make the sparklines:

- Decide on the data range you want to plot. To create a sparkline, go to Insert ➔ Sparklines ➔ Sparkline Type. I'm going to use Lines as an example for the time being.

- Select a range by clicking on the button. After selecting the range from the Excel button, press Enter & click OK to locate the sparklines' position. Determine how much space is required to accommodate the data source. There must be six rows in each position of a sparkline if your data source provides six rows.

You might attempt the following to format the sparkline:

For changing the color of markers:

- Sparkline Tools may be accessed by clicking on a cell in the sparkline.

- To alter the color of a certain marker, go to the Sparkline tool menu and choose the marker from the drop-down menu.

Example: High points are in green, low points are in red, and the rest are blue. Example:

For changing the width of your lines:

- Sparkline Tools may be accessed by clicking on a cell in the sparkline.

- To modify the width of a Sparkline line, go to the Sparkline Color ➔ Weight within the Sparkline tools contextual menu.

Excel 2013's Quick Analysis tool was a big time-saver when it was first launched. When you use this functionality, you may easily produce many types of graphs and charts with a single button click.

If you're using Excel 2013 or later, you'll see a new button in the lower-right corner of your chosen range called the Quick Analysis Excel Button.

If you choose "Quick Analysis," the following choices will appear:

- Sparklines

- Formatting

- Totals

- Charts

- Tables

After selecting an option, Excel will provide a view of the potential outcomes based on your data.

- If you go to charts and click over the Quick Analysis icon, you may rapidly construct the graph.

- The average value for every column may be rapidly inserted by selecting Totals and then inserting a row:

- You may easily insert Sparklines by clicking on Sparklines: See how simple it is to do a variety of visualizations and analyses with the Quick Analysis feature.

Data Reporting

Excel analytics data reporting demands more than accounting expertise; it also necessitates a complete understanding of Excel's features and the capability to improve the report's aesthetic appeal.

- Before making any changes to the Excel spreadsheet, disable Auto Refresh. Making changes to a worksheet will prevent the table from updating.

- Refresh the Xls Report Designer Tasks Pane and choose "Switch auto-refresh off" from the Refresh icon.

- The new row should be inserted into the layout by selecting a cell below where you wish to place it.

- Then, right-click and pick Insert ➜ Table Row Above from the context menu. Make careful to utilize the Table Delete methods like the Insert operations above when removing columns or rows.

- Select a cell within the table area of a column or row you wish to remove, and then press the delete key. After that, right-click and choose

- Delete from the context menu, after which you may choose between deleting Table Columns & Table Rows.

- Delete any columns or rows that aren't required. To make the table refresh faster, you should remove any unnecessary cells from its layout.

Here, you've just scratched the surface of what Excel can do. Using Excel analytics, you may play around with complicated data visualizations or arrange divergent statistics to uncover the endless variety of Excel features. Being proficient with Excel is an asset if you're interested in working in data analytics.

CHAPTER 7: EXCEL MACRO & VBA

Visual Basic for Applications (VBA) Macros allows users to develop their functions in Excel and automate repetitive manual chores. In addition, Microsoft Windows Application Programming Interface (API) may be accessed using VBA (API). Customizing toolbars, menus, dialogue boxes, and forms is one of the most common applications of this tool.

Use the form below to obtain instant access to our Excel VBA cheat sheet, which includes an overview of the most important codes & terminology, macros, and best practices.

Creating VBA Macros

The user must first create the Module file before they can begin coding. Several macros may be found in a single module file. Insert ➜ Module should be used to build a brand-new module. The properties panel in the bottom left quadrant of your editor allows the user to give this module a name. To add a new module, start typing its name and enter.

Naming VBA Macros

To begin, the macro should be assigned a distinctive name. This macro's name can't be confused with the names of any other macros or Excel properties, functions, or tools. To activate a macro, the user must type in the macro name.

In the editor's code window, write Sub name() and hit "enter" to create a macro name. Fill your window with the macro's general format by pressing Enter. CFI Macro, for example, may be named by typing in the command "Sub cfiMacro()" and pressing enter. Just a few lines underneath the "Sub," your VBA Editor would automatically add an "End Sub" line.

It is important to remember that function, VBA macro, or variable names should be written in lowercase if there are only one or two words and in uppercase for every additional work. VBA names are often not allowed to include spaces.

There are two words in CFI Macro; hence it should be spelled as "cfiMacro." It is significant to remember that these are only suggestions for best practices and are not legally required to be followed.

Sub Naming into VBA

The beginning of the macro code is shown by the Sub Name() line. The End Sub serves as a marker for the conclusion of the paragraph.

If the user decides to, he or she might create a new Sub Name () line beneath the first End Sub and construct a second macro. Excel will automatically draw a line between the two macros when you run this.

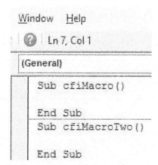

An Excel macro's fundamental structure looks like this.

The next stage is to specify the parameters the user will utilize in the code before diving into actual process coding.

7.1 ENABLING MACROS

To enable macros is to execute or run a macro in a certain file to reduce the time it takes to do the same task again.

Click the "allow all macros" checkbox in the "trust center" of the File tab's "settings" button to make macros available.

When a macro-enabled worksheet is opened, there is a chance that problems may be encountered.

As a result, macros from external sources are disabled in Excel because of security concerns.**Enabling Macros into Excel**

When activating macros, the user is primarily responsible for determining the scope of the permissions granted. Partial, full, or nil consent may be granted (no permission).

Excel macros may be activated by following the following steps:

- Click "options" within the File menu.

- You'll find the "trust center settings" option within the Excel options dialogue box.

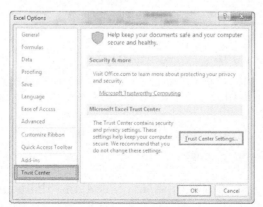

For "macro settings," choose how much access to provide. The user has the choice of selecting among the following alternatives (shown in the following graphic) based on their specific needs:

- No alerts are sent when "Disable all macros without notification" is selected.

- Using the "Disable all macros with notice" command, you may get alerts that all macros in the current file have been deactivated.

- Only digitally signed macros may be used when "Disable all macros excluding digitally signed macros" is selected.

- The command "Enable all macros" allows you to execute whatever macro you choose.

- The specified macro parameters may be applied by clicking "OK."

It's important to note that the option "allow all macros" only appears if the source can be trusted.

Select "Allow all controls without limits and without prompting" in the "ActiveX settings" option under "trust center settings."

To enable macros, ActiveX controls must be active. The purpose of macros necessitates certain controls.

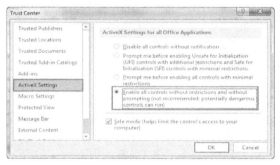

Enabling Macro Files Permanently

To use a VBA or macro content in a file acquired from a reputable source, the macros must be activated in the file. In some situations, the macros are permanently activated to save time.

Excel macros may be permanently enabled by following these steps:

- In the File menu, choose "options."

This option may be found in the "Excel Options" dialogue box under the "trust center" section.

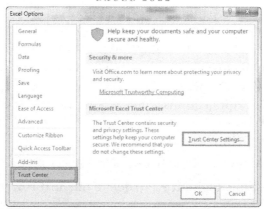

Step 3: Choose "Enable all macros" within the "macro settings" tab. The specified macro parameters may be applied by clicking "OK."

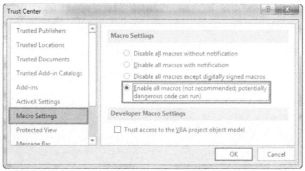

Alerts When Activating Macros

To use macros, the following things must be kept in mind:

- Save the file as a "macro-enabled workbook" if it contains VBA code. The VBA code is not saved when a file is saved with a different extension; hence, macros are not enabled.

- Enabling all macros has the effect of automatically running all macros. Macros from both trustworthy and untrusted sources may be enabled, which is a risk.

- To deactivate all macros with no indication, there is no explanation for why they are not functioning. If you want to see the warnings, pick the "disable all notification macros" option.

7.2 AUTOMATE RECURRING TASKS WITH VBA

One irritating thing is that very few people know that VBA programming allows you to automate incredibly repetitious processes.

Modifying a code is easy no matter what operation you try to automate. Breaking the code down line-by-line reveals how easy it is.

Here are some examples of how VBA coding might simplify your life.

To utilize VBA code in Excel, ensure that the Developer option is enabled in the application. Make sure you check the "Developer" checkbox in the Ribbon & Toolbar section of Excel's preferences before you can use it. To access Macros, go to the Developer tab and choose it.

While it is possible to record macros, editing the code is required to "generalize" them so that they may be used again, such as 100 times in a row.

In Microsoft Visuals Basic for Applications, you can simply copy & paste the code & save the changed macro by clicking Macros➜ Edit.

How can you Delete any Other Row?

Excel users sit for hours at a time, meticulously erasing every row.

You may erase one row at a time, then hit F4 to delete the next row you'd want to remove.

Excel's F4 shortcut allows you to repeat the previous action you took, but if you want to erase every other row, it will take a long time.

Suppose we wish to remove every single row in Spreadsheet 1000 times. The following is the code that we employ:

```
Sub Delete_Rows()

Dim i As Integer

For i = 1 To 1000
    ActiveCell.Offset(1, 0).Rows("1:1").EntireRow.Select
    Selection.Delete Shift:=xlUp
Next i

End Sub
```

Note that when executing the code, Excel's active cell should be placed in the upper left-hand corner or a single cell just above the cell you wish to begin removing.

Make a backup before using macros since this code will remove every row for the following 1000 times without regard to context.

Let's dissect this. The macro's name is Delete Rows. You create a new integer I and place it in a loop from one to ten thousand.

You remove the row one row underneath our current row in each of these loops.

After the first iteration is completed, it is repeated 999 times. In each cycle, variable I am raised by one step. After the macro is finished, you will have erased every row for thousand rows.

There may be times when this macro isn't enough for your needs. Instead of 1000, enter the desired number.

Instead of deleting every nth row, what if you wanted to do so? ActiveCell needs a "2" instead of a "1". Add the value of each row to offset(1, 0) so that you may remove them one by one.

This situation instructs Excel to shift 1 downward and 0 horizontally. Every third or fourth row may be deleted by replacing the number 1 with 2 or 3.

Notice that the integer is misaligned by one with the nth row you wish to remove. Be cautious. It's important to remember that removing every other row also deletes the row after it.

To see it yourself, create a simple Excel spreadsheet with a few numbers and play about it to notice that every second, third, etc., the number would be deleted.

How can you Delete any Other Column?

Excel's additional columns may now be deleted using the following code:

```
Sub Delete_Columns()

Dim i As Integer

For i = 1 To 20
    ActiveCell.Offset(0, 1).Columns("A:A").EntireColumn.Select
    Selection.Delete Shift:=xlToLeft
Next i

End Sub
```

They're all the same notions. We decided to limit the loop to 20 repetitions this time around. Moving a single column to the right is now possible as opposed to the previous option of (1,0). As a bonus, the loop's final code uses x1ToLeft rather than x1Up.

Remember that you may alter the number of times this code iterates by altering the value of i. In addition, you may eliminate every third or fourth column, for example, by changing the parameter (0, 1) to, say, (0, 2) or (0, 3), respectively.

The number within the parameter is one fewer than the number of columns you would eliminate. 1 will remove all the columns in the second row; 2 will remove all the columns in the third row; and so on.

VBA code can be used to start filling a column using Excel with many values, such as 100,000.

Have you ever had to enter 100000 entries into an Excel spreadsheet?

You can keep counting by dragging a column down, but it takes a long time.

Only if you're filling with an adjoining column that has already been filled may you double-click the bottom-right section of a cell. Make any code that will begin counting from 1,2,3 up to 100,000. While Excel 2007 can only support 64000 rows, newer Excel versions allow you to create as many rows or columns as you like if the computer has enough RAM.

```
Sub Counting()
    ActiveCell.FormulaR1C1 = "1"
    ActiveCell.Offset(1, 0).Range("A1").Select
    ActiveCell.FormulaR1C1 = "2"
    ActiveCell.Offset(-1, 0).Range("A1:A2").Select
    Selection.AutoFill Destination:=ActiveCell.Range("A1:A100000"), Type:
        xlFillDefault
End Sub
```

What is the purpose of this VBA program? As a result, you currently have one column that goes from 1 up to 100000, filling the cells below us with "1," "2," and "3," respectively.

A new number or a different method of counting to 100000 is possible by changing the value you enter. Any desired value can be substituted for the default value of 1000000. To count in multiples of three, simply substitute "3" and "6" for "1" and "2," respectively.

Alternatively, you may write it in a simpler way like this:

```
Sub Counting()

For i = 1 To 100000
    Cells(i, 1).Value = i
Next i

End Sub
```

If you keep looping, the counter will keep going up by one.

To increase by 2s instead of 1s, replace I with I+I * 1; however, remember that this will necessitate a slight modification to the code.

If you want to measure in various steps, you can adjust the number I get multiplied by. To count in multiples of 4, use I + I * 3, for example.

7.3 DATA ENTRY FORM WITH VBA

A user form is used to input the data into an Excel database and then updated using VBA code in an Excel workbook. I've constructed a user form that includes the following fields: Id, Name, Email, Phone, Gender, Location, and Remarks. The following chapter displays the user form design. How to automate your project with VBA is explained in full in the following steps.

How do you create an Excel Workbook Data Entry User form? Let's look and find out!

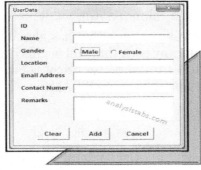

The KEY stages to creating this Data Entry Userform:

- In this example, you'll walk through how to build a data input user form throughout Excel using VBA.

- Let's elaborate on the procedure of creating such a Data entry user form. To write many procedures, you will use the following method.

- You'll employ several variables and objects as part of your routines.

- Step 2: Disable auto-update and events on the screen: Screen flickering and application events are temporarily disabled. In the initial stages of the procedure, you can use this.

- Creating a user form is the third step. Use your insert menu for adding the user form. Use the toolbox to add the necessary controls to the user form.

- Step 4: Develop a field validation procedure: The user must provide us with the correct data format. Your Data Worksheet must be validated before being updated. We begin the procedure when the user clicks on the "Add" button. In other words, whenever a user enters data, you check together all fields (Textboxes & radiobuttons) for validity.

- To find the last row, you need to write a function. A new function (fn LastRow) has been created to discover the last row within the data Worksheet and update data using a user form.

- A mechanism for erasing user form fields should be developed in Step 6. Data Worksheet columns A through G will be cleared using the technique (Clear DataSheet).

- To keep your spreadsheet up to date, follow these Create steps. Add or edit data in the Data Worksheet using a procedure (cmdAdd Click).

- Step 8: Create a procedure to remove the user from memory: CommandCancel Click can be used to quit a user form. To remove the user form, click on the 'cancel' button in the window's top right corner.

- Screen updates and events can now be enabled: Let's restart the application's screen updates and events. After the procedure, you can use this.

Designing Data Entry Userform:

In the next section, you'll examine your Data Entry UserForm project's control properties & values.

Control	Property	Value
UserForm	Name	frmData
	Caption	UserData
Label	Name	lblId
	Caption	ID
Label	Name	lblName
	Caption	Name
Label	Name	lblGender
	Caption	Gender
Label	Name	lblEAddr
	Caption	Email Address
Label	Name	lblCNum
	Caption	Contact Numer
Label	Name	lblRemarks
	Caption	Remarks
OptionButton	Name	obMale
	Caption	Male
	GroupNmae	g1
OptionButton	Name	obFMale
	Caption	FeMale
	GroupNmae	g1
TextBox	Name	txtId
	Enabled	FALSE
TextBox	Name	txtName
TextBox	Name	txtLocation
TextBox	Name	txtEAddr
TextBox	Name	txtCNum
TextBox	Name	txtRemarks
	MultiLine	TRUE
CommandButton	Name	cmdClear
	Caption	Clear
CommandButton	Name	cmdAdd
	Caption	Add
CommandButton	Name	cmdCancel
	Caption	Cancel

This is the Data Entry UserForm style that Was created. The form will take on the appearance shown below if all the control's properties and values are altered in the manner described above.

Code and Explanation:

Initialize global variables that will be used throughout the project.

```
' Variable declaration
Dim txtId, txtName, GenderValue, txtLocation, txtCNum, txtEAddr, txtRemarks
Dim iCnt As Integer
```

Disable the Screen Updating & Disable Events to prevent screen flickering and popups from interrupting your work.

```
With Application
    .ScreenUpdating = False
    .EnableEvents = False
End With
```

Add controls from the Toolbox to the user form to create a user form. Seven Labels, 2 Radio buttons, 6 Textboxes, and 3 CommandButtons will be used in this project. Use the design elements of the Data input user form to develop your user form.

A method for field validation must be developed in Step 4.

Before updating our Data Worksheet, you must ensure that the data is correct. As a result, you must collect data in the right format from the user. When the people click on the "Add" button, you begin the procedure. In other words, whenever a user enters data, you check all fields (radio buttons & Textboxes) for validity.

```
'Variable Declaration
Dim BlnVal As Boolean

' Check all the data(except remarks field) has entered are not on the userform
Sub Data_Validation()
    If txtName = "" Then
        MsgBox "Enter Name!", vbInformation, "Name"
        Exit Sub
    ElseIf frmData.obMale = False And frmData.obFMale = False Then
        MsgBox "Select Gender!", vbInformation, "Gender"
        Exit Sub
    ElseIf txtLocation = "" Then
        MsgBox "Enter Location!", vbInformation, "Location"
        Exit Sub
    ElseIf txtEAddr = "" Then
        MsgBox "Enter Address!", vbInformation, "Email Address"
        Exit Sub
    ElseIf txtCNum = "" Then
        MsgBox "Enter Contact Number!", vbInformation, "Contact Number"
        Exit Sub
    Else
        BlnVal = 1
    End If
End Sub
```

The function to discover the final row is the fifth step.

You may get the final row in a Data Worksheet using this function code below. Alternatively, you may supply the name of a sheet into the method as an argument to have it return the last row of that sheet.

```
'In this example we are finding the last Row of specified Sheet
Function fn_LastRow(ByVal Sht As Worksheet)

    Dim lastRow As Long
    lastRow = Sht.Cells.SpecialCells(xlLastCell).Row
    lRow = Sht.Cells.SpecialCells(xlLastCell).Row
    Do While Application.CountA(Sht.Rows(lRow)) = 0 And lRow <> 1
        lRow = lRow - 1
    Loop
    fn_LastRow = lRow
End Function
```

Step 5.1: Design a mechanism for erasing user form fields.

To clear your Userform fields, use the following code. Such a feature helps when you need to change more than 1 record at a time. The UserForm is ready for new data when you add a new record to a worksheet, then clear the data fields.

```
'Clearing data fields of userform
Private Sub cmdClear_Click()
    Application.ScreenUpdating = False
        txtId.Text = ""
        txtName.Text = ""
        obMale.Value = True
        txtLocation = ""
        txtEAddr = ""
        txtCNum = ""
        txtRemarks = ""
    Application.ScreenUpdating = True
End Sub
```

Step 5.2: Create a procedure to update data to the Worksheet.

Here is the code to add or update data to the Worksheet.

```vba
Sub cmdAdd_Click()
    On Error GoTo ErrOccured
    'Boolean Value
    BlnVal = 0

    'Data Validation
    Call Data_Validation

    'Check validation of all fields are completed are not
    If BlnVal = 0 Then Exit Sub

    'TurnOff screen updating
    With Application
       .ScreenUpdating = False
       .EnableEvents = False
    End With

    'Variable declaration
    Dim txtId, txtName, GenderValue, txtLocation, txtCNum, txtEAddr, txtRemarks
    Dim iCnt As Integer

    'find next available row to update data in the data worksheet
    iCnt = fn_LastRow(Sheets("Data")) + 1

    'Find Gender value
    If frmData.obMale = True Then
       GenderValue = "Male"
    Else
       GenderValue = "Female"
    End If

    'Update userform data to the Data Worksheet
    With Sheets("Data")
       .Cells(iCnt, 1) = iCnt - 1
       .Cells(iCnt, 2) = frmData.txtName
       .Cells(iCnt, 3) = GenderValue
       .Cells(iCnt, 4) = frmData.txtLocation.Value
       .Cells(iCnt, 5) = frmData.txtEAddr
       .Cells(iCnt, 6) = frmData.txtCNum
       .Cells(iCnt, 7) = frmData.txtRemarks

       'Diplay headers on the first row of Data Worksheet
       If .Range("A1") = "" Then
          .Cells(1, 1) = "Id"
          .Cells(1, 2) = "Name"
          .Cells(1, 3) = "Gender"
          .Cells(1, 4) = "Location"
          .Cells(1, 5) = "Email Addres"
          .Cells(1, 6) = "Contact Number"
          .Cells(1, 7) = "Remarks"

          'Formatiing Data
          .Columns("A:G").Columns.AutoFit
          .Range("A1:G1").Font.Bold = True
          .Range("A1:G1").LineStyle = xlDash

       End If
    End With

    'Display next available Id number on the Userform
    'Variable declaration
    Dim IdVal As Integer

    'Finding last row in the Data Sheet
    IdVal = fn_LastRow(Sheets("Data"))

    'Update next available id on the userform
    frmData.txtId = IdVal

ErrOccured:
    'TurnOn screen updating
    Application.ScreenUpdating = True
    Application.EnableEvents = True
                             130
End Sub
```

A process to empty the user form is needed in step 6.

Here is your code to leave from the user form. You may also click on the upper right corner of a user interface.

```
'Exit from the Userform
Private Sub cmdCancel_Click()
    Unload Me
End Sub
```

Ending the project by enabling or turning on Screen Update & Events.

```
With Application
    .ScreenUpdating = True
    .EnableEvents = True
End With
```

Final VBA's Module Code (Macro):

These instructions are for creating a Data Entry UserForm project, as shown below. Add your following code to a Userform(FrmData) by double-clicking it.

```
'Variable Declaration
Dim BlnVal As Boolean

Private Sub UserForm_Initialize()
    'Variable declaration
    Dim IdVal As Integer

    'Finding last row in the Data Sheet
    IdVal = fn_LastRow(Sheets("Data"))

    'Update next available id on the userform
    frmData.txtId = IdVal
End Sub
Sub cmdAdd_Click()
    On Error GoTo ErrOccured
    'Boolean Value
    BlnVal = 0

    'Data Validation
    Call Data_Validation

    'Check validation of all fields are completed are not
    If BlnVal = 0 Then Exit Sub

    'TurnOff screen updating
    With Application
        .ScreenUpdating = False
        .EnableEvents = False
    End With
```

```vba
'Variable declaration
Dim txtId, txtName, GenderValue, txtLocation, txtCNum, txtEAddr, txtRemarks
Dim iCnt As Integer

'find next available row to update data in the data worksheet
iCnt = fn_LastRow(Sheets("Data")) + 1


'Find Gender value
If frmData.obMale = True Then
  GenderValue = "Male"
Else
  GenderValue = "Female"
End If


'Update userform data to the Data Worksheet
With Sheets("Data")
    .Cells(iCnt, 1) = iCnt - 1
    .Cells(iCnt, 2) = frmData.txtName
    .Cells(iCnt, 3) = GenderValue
    .Cells(iCnt, 4) = frmData.txtLocation.Value
    .Cells(iCnt, 5) = frmData.txtEAddr
    .Cells(iCnt, 6) = frmData.txtCNum
    .Cells(iCnt, 7) = frmData.txtRemarks



    'Diplay headers on the first row of Data Worksheet
    If .Range("A1") = "" Then
        .Cells(1, 1) = "Id"
        .Cells(1, 2) = "Name"
        .Cells(1, 3) = "Gender"
        .Cells(1, 4) = "Location"
        .Cells(1, 5) = "Email Addres"
        .Cells(1, 6) = "Contact Number"
        .Cells(1, 7) = "Remarks"

    'Formatiing Data
    .Columns("A:G").Columns.AutoFit
    .Range("A1:G1").Font.Bold = True
    .Range("A1:G1").LineStyle = xlDash


    End If
End With
```

```vba
'Display next available Id number on the Userform
'Variable declaration
    Dim IdVal As Integer

    'Finding last row in the Data Sheet
    IdVal = fn_LastRow(Sheets("Data"))

    'Update next available id on the userform
    frmData.txtId = IdVal
ErrOccured:
    'TurnOn screen updating
    Application.ScreenUpdating = True
    Application .EnableEvents = True

End Sub

'In this example we are finding the last Row of specified Sheet
Function fn_LastRow(ByVal Sht As Worksheet)

    Dim lastRow As Long
    lastRow = Sht.Cells.SpecialCells(xlLastCell).Row
    lRow = Sht.Cells.SpecialCells(xlLastCell).Row
    Do While Application.CountA(Sht.Rows(lRow)) = 0 And lRow <> 1
        lRow = lRow - 1
    Loop
    fn_LastRow = lRow

End Function

'Exit from the Userform
Private Sub cmdCancel_Click()
    Unload Me
End Sub

' Check all the data(except remarks field) has entered are not on the userform
Sub Data_Validation()
    If txtName = "" Then
        MsgBox "Enter Name!", vbInformation, "Name"
        Exit Sub
    ElseIf frmData.obMale = False And frmData.obFMale = False Then
        MsgBox "Select Gender!", vbInformation, "Gender"
        Exit Sub
    ElseIf txtLocation = "" Then
        MsgBox "Enter Location!", vbInformation, "Location"
        Exit Sub
    ElseIf txtEAddr = "" Then
        MsgBox "Enter Address!", vbInformation, "Email Address"
        Exit Sub
    ElseIf txtCNum = "" Then
        MsgBox "Enter Contact Number!", vbInformation, "Contact Number"
        Exit Sub
    Else
        BlnVal = 1
    End If
End Sub
```

```
'Clearing data fields of userform
Private Sub cmdClear_Click()
    Application.ScreenUpdating = False
        txtId.Text = ""
        txtName.Text = ""
        obMale.Value = True
        txtLocation = ""
        txtEAddr = ""
        txtCNum = ""
        txtRemarks = ""
    Application.ScreenUpdating = True
End Sub
```

Add the below code for your newly created module, which you can access using the Insert Module menu item.

```
'Here is the code to Show Data Entry UserForm
Sub Oval2_Click()
    frmData.Show
End Sub
'To clear data columns data on Data Worksheet
Sub Clear_DataSheet()
    Sheets("Data").Columns("A:G").Clear
End Sub
```

Worksheet Data Entry UserForm Displayed:

A 'Data Entry User Form' may be created following these steps.

- Selecting insert from the drawings group in the insert menu may insert whatever form you choose.

- It's simple: Right-click a shape and choose "assign macro."

- Click OK after selecting 'Oval2 Click' from the list of potential macro names.

- Navigate now to the Developers section.

- The Controls group should be unchecked to disable Design Mode.

- Return to the shape and choose your Data Entry UserForm by clicking the produced shape in the current Workbook's Worksheet.

Instructions for Executing the Procedure:

You may examine the code in the attached file and then run it. Using the code to build a new workbook and then testing it is also possible. To put the code above into action, follow these steps.

- Press Alt+F11 to bring up the VBA Editor window.

- Using the Insert menu, create a new module.

- Paste the given instructions into the new module.

- You may access your Data Entry UserForm by pressing the F5 key on your keyboard or selecting 'Show Data Entry UserForm!' from the Data Worksheet.

The outcome of your project:

For convenience, below is a picture of the product.

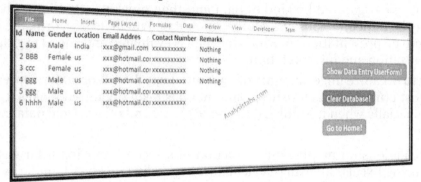

CONCLUSION

Excel is the industry standard for database programs often used for data input, budgeting, and money management. Like every other piece of software, Microsoft Excel has its flaws. Once you've purchased a certificate, consider the upsides and downsides to determine if Excel is the right choice for you. One of the most fundamental uses for MS Excel is for data organizing and collecting.

Information may be organized by kind of data and then quickly sorted into tidy columns and rows. Although it may be difficult to observe a large amount of data in its raw form, the program's resources allow users to create presentations in which the data is evaluated and added to graphs, charts, or tables for better visualization and interpretation.

Excel's ability to organize huge amounts of data into logical, well-organized spreadsheets and graphs is one of its most crucial characteristics. Data that has been organized makes it much easier to read and analyze, especially when it is utilized to create charts and other visual data interpretations.

Excel does calculations on numbers in a fraction of a second, making it far easier to perform bulk computations using Excel than using a calculator. Depending on one's familiarity with Excel and level of expertise working with the program, formulas and computations may be utilized to efficiently calculate simple and complex equations by using huge volumes of data. There are several entry-level positions for which excel is a necessary ability, like Personal Assistant, Admin Aide, Bookkeeper/Project Manager, and so on. You should take Excel if you want a better chance of getting a job; thus, it makes sense to do so!

Excel is a must-have tool for every company, and it's no surprise it's so popular. You will never run out of things to learn with Excel, no matter how much experience you have. Excel will never tire you, and you'll be thrilled by its strength and what you discover about it regularly.

Speeding efficiency and making employees more effective when dealing with big data and computations are critical to Excel's success. Excel's more advanced functions help you finish your tasks and analyze your data more rapidly when you understand the program better. Makes it possible to keep teammates updated on data, which may help simplify workflows.

Advanced Excel skills will also help you speed up your computations. Repetitive computations consume a lot of time, particularly when you double-check the work. Complex computations may be performed using Excel's more powerful features. Using computer software to execute the computations saves more time for other duties and ensures that you get correct data the first time, making it a win-win situation for everyone involved.

The advantages do not stop here; begin using Microsoft Excel and educate yourself on your own.

💣A GIFT FOR YOU (DOWNLOAD IT) 💣

SCAN THE QR CODE BELOW and get:

Bonus 1: Top 30 Excel Interview Questions for 2023 (Beginner to Advanced)

Bonus 2: The Top 5 Mistakes everybody makes when using Excel and why they are stopping you from advancing your Excel level.

Bonus 3: The #1 Secret that I used to quickly advance my Excel skills

Made in the USA
Coppell, TX
15 June 2023

18118872R00077